CIVIL DEFENSE IN THE NUCLEAR AGE

CIVIL DEFENSE IN THE NUCLEAR AGE

BY ELAINE K. ANDREWS

FRANKLIN WATTS
NEW YORK | LONDON | TORONTO | SYDNEY | 1985
AN IMPACT BOOK

Lourdes High School Library
4034 West 56th Street
Chicago, Illinois 60629

Photographs courtesy of:
UPI/Bettmann Archive: opposite p. 1,
pp. 7, 10, 18, 23, 28, 33, 40, 51, 60;
AP/Wide World: p. 77.

Library of Congress Cataloging in Publication Data

Andrews, Elaine K.
Civil defense in the nuclear age.

(An Impact book)
Bibliography: p.
Includes index.
Summary: Examines the issues and questions
posed by civil defense in the nuclear age
and the related controversy over the arms
race and the nuclear freeze movement.
   1. Nuclear warfare—Juvenile literature. 2. United
States—Civil defense—Juvenile literature. 3. Soviet
Union—Civil defense—Juvenile literature. 4. Nuclear
arms control—Juvenile literature. 5. Disarmament—
Juvenile literature. [1. Nuclear warfare. 2. United
States—Civil defense. 3. Soviet Union—Civil defense.
4. Nuclear arms control. 5. Disarmament] I. Title.
U263.A53 1985   363.3'5   84-22099
ISBN 0-531-04853-5

Copyright © 1985 by Elaine K. Andrews
All rights reserved
Printed in the United States of America
5 4 3 2 1

CONTENTS

INTRODUCTION
1

THINKING ABOUT THE UNTHINKABLE
4

THE PLIGHT OF THE NONCOMBATANT
13

THE NUCLEAR AGE ARRIVES
27

ON THE DRAWING BOARD—
CIVIL DEFENSE AT HOME AND ABROAD
57

CAN CIVIL DEFENSE WORK?
83

THE FUTURE OF CIVIL DEFENSE
96

FOR FURTHER INFORMATION
99

INDEX
101

CIVIL DEFENSE IN THE NUCLEAR AGE

INTRODUCTION

When primitive people were first frightened by thunder and lightning and fled to their caves for protection, they were practicing an early kind of civil defense. People have always tried to protect themselves from the forces of nature—and the forces of war.

In the modern sense civil defense is the planned, organized systems set up by people or their governments to help themselves and each other in times of emergencies. Such emergencies include natural catastrophes such as floods, tornadoes, and earthquakes. They also include a catastrophe made only by human beings themselves—war.

It was not until the twentieth century that governments began to think seriously about protecting their civilian populations from the ravages of war. During the centuries before that, civilians in the path of war were expected to take care of themselves.

Warring armies had little regard for those who did not fight. Civilians who got in the way usually perished along with the soldiers.

During two terrible world wars, governments began to devise ways to protect civilians. Civil defense as a national policy in wartime was established. In World War I (1914–18) civil defense efforts were minimal. Sirens were used to warn people in cities that an air attack was coming, and they were expected to take cover. For those in the countryside, whose homes and land became a battlefield, about all they could do was flee. By the time of World War II (1939–45), governments were better prepared to protect civilians. Shelters and warning systems had been devised, and people were better organized to help themselves and each other. At the end of World War II, it was generally recognized that civil defense had played a key role in saving lives.

Out of World War II, however, came a new threat to consider in civil defense planning—nuclear weapons. Two Japanese cities had been destroyed in a flash, each by a single atomic bomb. The world was stunned by this terrible new weapon. Still, people did not immediately ask whether there was any protection from such a force.

The United States had developed and used the first atomic bombs. By 1949, however, the Soviet Union also had atomic bombs. Now there was a reason for Americans to think about self-protection, as the two superpowers confronted each other in a clash of ideologies and in an arms race that escalated with each passing decade.

From the 1950s to our own time, Americans have been divided over the issue of civil defense in a nuclear age. Some insist that a strong civil defense system can be effective in saving lives in a nuclear war. They want to develop strong civil defense measures as part of our total national security. Others believe civil defense is useless in a nuclear attack. They argue that a massive civil defense system will lull Americans into thinking that a nuclear war is survivable.

The debate over civil defense in the United States is closely linked to the debate about the arms race and the nuclear-freeze movement. The civil defense debate may not be resolved quickly. But a study of the issues and questions on both sides is important to an understanding of the direction our nation may take in the future.

THINKING ABOUT THE UNTHINKABLE

The Office of Technology Assessment (OTA) is a government agency that regularly analyzes the state of the nation's technology. In 1979, at the request of a congressional committee on civil defense, the OTA compiled a report entitled *The Effects of Nuclear War,* which estimated the consequences of all-out nuclear attacks on the United States and the Soviet Union. The agency concluded that during the first thirty days following an attack 165 million Americans would die and around 100 million Russians. (The population of the United States is about 227 million; the Soviet Union is around 270 million.) These figures do not include those who would die from their injuries or from the disruption of the economic system—the lack of food and medical supplies, no transportation or distribution facilities, banks and businesses destroyed. The study concluded that the survivors would return to "the economic equivalent of the Middle Ages."

ONE AMERICAN CITY: DETROIT

The OTA's report dealt not only with the effects of a nuclear war on the entire United States, but it focused on individual cities as well.

Detroit, with a population of 4.3 million, is the fifth-largest city in the nation. The OTA used Detroit as representative of high-density areas to estimate civilian casualties as the result of a one-megaton ground explosion, a one-megaton air explosion, and a twenty-five-megaton air explosion. Here are the figures: a one-megaton ground explosion—220,000 dead and 420,000 injured; a one-megaton air explosion—470,000 dead and 630,000 injured; a twenty-five-megaton air explosion—1,840,000 dead and 1,360,000 injured. These figures do not include the injuries or deaths from fallout.

Going further, the agency described the topographic effects of a one-megaton ground explosion. In downtown Detroit a crater 200 feet (61 m) deep and 1,000 feet (305 m) wide would be dug out. A mass of radioactive dirt about 2,000 feet (610 m) wide would surround the crater. Within about 2 miles (3.2 km) of ground zero (the center of the explosion) no buildings would remain standing. Just about all the people within that radius would be killed. Proceeding farther out from ground zero, the walls of buildings would be completely blown out from about 2 to 3 miles (3.2–4.8 km). Many people would be killed by the collapsing buildings. Still farther out, the contents of buildings would be blown onto the streets, and low buildings would be destroyed from about 3 to 5 miles (4.8–8 km). Fires would start and spread rapidly.

Continuing outward, about 25 percent

of the people would be injured, but few would be killed outright from about 5 to 8 miles (8–12.9 km. Depending on weather conditions, fires could spread rapidly in this area. Between 3,000 and 75,000 people would be badly enough burned to require treatment in a burn center. In 1977 there were only eighty-five burn centers in the entire nation. All of them could handle only 1,000 to 2,000 patients.

The direction of the wind would determine how many people would die as the result of radioactive fallout. If the wind were blowing from the southwest toward Detroit, fallout would be carried into Canada, which is less heavily populated than the areas south of Detroit. Estimating a wind from the northwest at 15 miles (24 km) an hour, the agency reckoned that fallout would be carried as far south as Pittsburgh.

The study also took into account the doses of radiation that people would accumulate over a seven-day period. In the Detroit area and for about a 50-mile (81-km) radius, the dose would be 3,000 rems. By the time the fallout got to Cleveland, the dose would be 900 rems. As the wind carried the fallout farther south, the dose would lessen. In the Pittsburgh area, the dose would be 90 rems. Fifty percent of the people exposed to a dose of 250 to 450 rems over a seven-day period would die from radiation sickness.

The study goes on to discuss the lack of medical and health facilities, since these would be destroyed in the Detroit area. Transportation and communications systems would be destroyed. Help from outside would be hampered because of the

In 1979, the Office of Technology Assessment used Detroit as representative of high-density areas to estimate civilian casualties in a nuclear war.

contamination from the fallout and the lack of transportation. Even if the injured were gotten out of the city, where could 420,000 injured people be sent? (At that time the United States had only about 1.5 million hospital beds.)

By speculating on possible effects of a nuclear attack on one American city, civil defense planners were better able to anticipate what problems could arise and what steps could be taken to save lives.

HIROSHIMA AND NAGASAKI
We don't have to get all our information on nuclear war from hypothetical situations, however. A real and terrible attack took place in August 1945, when the United States bombed the Japanese cities of Hiroshima and Nagasaki. Each city was devastated by a single atomic bomb. The effects of these bombings are still being studied.

Beginning in 1944, the United States carried out devastating aerial raids on Japanese cities. At first the raids were on industry and transportation facilities. Later, in an effort to force a Japanese surrender, bombing raids concentrated on cities and their civilian populations. Japan had a civil defense system of air-raid shelters, warning sirens, and air-raid wardens. But Japanese cities were crowded, and most buildings were wooden and highly flammable. The raids carried out against Tokyo and other cities caused massive damage through firestorms. One raid on Tokyo alone left nearly 84,000 dead, 41,000 injured, and a million people homeless. By the end of the war, ninety-eight Japanese cities had been bombed from the air or shelled by warships.

Then, on the morning of August 6, 1945, the nuclear age began. Around seven o'clock, an air-raid warning signal sounded over the city of Hiroshima. When it was discovered that the plane overhead was only a U.S. weather plane, the all-clear was sounded. An hour later, Japanese spotters saw two B-29 bombers heading toward Tokyo. The radio station broadcast a warning but announced that the planes seemed to be on a reconnaissance mission. People were told to take shelter, but since most were already at work or on their way to work, they ignored the advice.

At 8:15, there was a blinding flash as the bomb—called Little Boy—exploded 1,000 feet (305 m) above the city. Its force was equal to 20,000 tons of TNT. Within an instant, the fireball from the explosion reached a temperature of several million degrees. As the fireball widened, it raised the temperature of the ground beneath it to roughly 5,000 degrees. The heat from this fireball was intense enough to burn people who were more than 2 miles (3.2 km) from the blast. Along with the heat, the blast caused a stunning shock wave that shot out from the center. Everything within 1.25 miles (2 km) of the blast center was demolished by the shock wave, which was followed by a hurricane-force wind that hurled people through the air.

Thousands died instantly from the heat or the force of the blast. Thousands more were severely injured. A heavy cloud of dust and smoke spread over the city, and hundreds of fires broke out. Those who could fled to a large private park that was untouched by the immediate effects of the bomb. Others threw themselves into the

Little Boy, the bomb detonated over Hiroshima in 1945, was only 28 inches (71 cm) in diameter and 120 inches (305 cm) long, but its force was equal to 20,000 tons of TNT.

city's river to escape the fires that raged out of control. As people made their way to hospitals, it became obvious that the surviving medical personnel could not cope with the injuries. Ten thousand people crowded into Hiroshima's best hospital, where doctors soon realized they could do little if anything to treat the terrible burns.

In a city of 240,000 as many as 140,000 people died on the day of the attack or within a few weeks. Three days after the attack on Hiroshima, another bomb was dropped on Nagasaki. It is estimated that 70,000 people died in that raid or shortly afterward.

The aftereffects of the atomic bombs continue to linger on. A report compiled by Japanese specialists attributes 130,000 more deaths five years after the raids to the effects of the atomic bombs. Recent research shows that around 370,000 survivors of the bombings continue to die slowly. Survivors of Hiroshima are known as *hibakusha*, or explosion-affected people. Statistics show that they have up to five times as many physical ailments as the rest of the population. They are hospitalized for an average of sixty-five days a year, and their life span is sixty-four years compared with the Japanese average of seventy-four. The majority of *hibakusha* have cancer or cardiovascular ailments. The children of *hibakusha* women were often born with physical defects or later suffered leukemia or mental retardation. Because of physical deformity many of these survivors lead solitary lives, and their poor physical condition makes many of them unemployable. Psychiatrists also note that many suffer from a sense of guilt or shame at being alive. The Japanese government provides free medical care and a monthly cash allowance of about eighty dollars. But many survivors feel this is not enough. Some have turned to crime, and many are bitter over what they feel is their government's lack of compensation.

To understand the problems facing civil defense officials in an all-out nuclear war, one has to think of what happened at Hiroshima and Nagasaki. The equivalent of 20,000 tons of TNT exploded over Hiroshima. Today the yield of all the nuclear weapons in the world is equal to about 20 billion tons of TNT. That is more than 1.5 million times greater than the bomb that destroyed Hiroshima.

THE PLIGHT OF THE NONCOMBATANT

Organized civil defense did not really begin until the twentieth century. Before that, rulers and governments made little or no effort to protect civilians caught up in their nations' military conflicts.

DEFENSELESS CIVILIANS

Long ago, empires rose and fell as armies roamed the Mediterranean world, conquering territories, cities, and people. For civilians who got in the way of these armies, the "choice" was usually enslavement or death.

Ancient cities were particularly unsafe for civilians. These cities were often walled and fortified, and civilians could and did take refuge in them. But if a city was besieged—and taken—civilians were seldom spared. The biblical city of Jericho is an example. Jericho—the capital of the Canaanite people—lay on the western side of the Jordan River in the southeastern part of what is now Israel. According to the

Bible, an Israelite army besieged the city. When Jericho finally fell, the victorious Israelites put the entire city to the sword—men and women, young and old.

One of the most famous sieges of history is that of the city of Troy by the Greeks in the ninth century B.C. According to the *Iliad,* by the Greek poet Homer, the city was besieged for several years. When the Greek army finally succeeded in overcoming Troy's defenses and poured into the city, the people were killed and the city plundered. Those who survived were taken as slaves.

Another ancient city that fell to a conquering army was Carthage, the capital of the empire of Carthage. In 149 B.C. the armies of Rome laid siege to this city on the Mediterranean coast of North Africa. After three years, the city fell. Most of the people were slaughtered, and the rest were sold into slavery. The Romans razed the city. Centuries later, in A.D. 410, Rome itself was plundered by invaders from the north.

During the Middle Ages in Europe, civilians caught in the path of warring armies could seek the protection of their own soldiers or they could try to flee from enemy forces. Neither choice was very promising. All armies lived off the land, and they pillaged the countryside and towns for food and supplies. For most civilians flight was not possible, mainly because there were few safe places to go. Like the cities of ancient times, medieval walled cities offered some protection. But also as in ancient times, civilians caught in a besieged city could usually expect to be slaughtered along with its defenders.

As time passed, weapons became more deadly. Guns were first introduced into Europe around the beginning of the 1400s, and over the centuries they were improved upon. By the 1600s armies were hauling cannons around with them, and soldiers were carrying crude but dangerous muskets. Now cannons could smash city walls and spray fire and explosives on the hapless citizens. Cities were becoming more and more vulnerable, offering even less protection than in earlier times.

For civilians war was a catastrophe over which they had little control and from which they had little protection. The plight of civilians in warfare can be seen in one of Europe's most savage conflicts—the Thirty Years War. From 1618 to 1648, European armies—French, Polish, Italian, Spanish, Swedish, Austrian, German—fought a ruthless religious and territorial war, for the most part on German soil. The countryside was devastated, whole populations were decimated, and cities and towns lay in ruins. Industry and commerce all but stopped. Plague and hunger raged, and wolves roamed the empty streets of once-thriving towns and villages. Sixteen years into the war, half of Germany's population was gone—killed in the war or dead from disease. Historians estimate that it took Germany 200 years to recover from the ravages of the Thirty Years War.

During the war, civilian refugees wandered the countryside. Sometimes they attached themselves to one army or another for protection. Sometimes they fled to cities, which were then destroyed by besieging armies. The struggle of civilians to stay alive in this war was depicted by the twentieth-century German playwright Bertolt Brecht in *Mother Courage and Her Children*. In the play the homeless Mother Courage and her children roam the desolate German countryside with a peddler's cart. They go from army to army, selling whatever food and scraps of clothing they can pick up. Her sons are snatched up by one army or another and killed in battle; her daughter is murdered by marauding soldiers. In the end, Mother Courage harnesses herself to her cart and journeys on alone, following yet another army.

Even as weapons became more sophisticated and more destructive, nations made little effort to protect their civilian populations. Wars raged in eighteenth-century Europe and spread to the New World. Americans fought a revolution and later a bloody civil war. And civilians were still caught in the middle.

During the American Civil War (1861–65), people in the South suffered heavily. When Northern forces successfully invaded the South, they caused great damage and created thousands of civilian refugees. In their strategy to capture Southern armies, Northern forces pushed ruthlessly into Virginia, Tennessee, and Georgia. Union General William T. Sherman had once said that war is hell, and he set out to prove it. In 1864 his army marched from Tennessee to Georgia, destroying everything in its path. People abandoned their farms and homes and fled as he advanced southward to Atlanta, then a city of about 10,000. He laid siege to and mercilessly bombarded the nearly defenseless city. Southern troops abandoned Atlanta to its fate. As they moved out, thousands of panicked civilians followed in their wake, clogging the roads to the south. Once the city was captured, Sherman set fire to it and began his famous march to the sea across Georgia to Savannah. Stating that his objective was the "utter destruction of [Georgia's] roads, houses and people," he and his troops marched on. Living off the land as it advanced, Sherman's army cut a path 50 miles (80 km) wide and 300 miles (483 km) long. He took Savannah four days before Christmas, 1864, and presented the city to President Abraham Lincoln as a holiday gift.

There are no exact figures on the civilian casualties in the Civil War, but thousands of Southerners were uprooted from their homes and their land and left to fend for themselves. Thousands more were killed or maimed through the violence of war. One thing is certain: for those civilians caught in the path of the war, if they escaped with their lives, they lost just about everything else.

Unorganized and defenseless, civilians continued to be victimized by the ravages of war.

WAR IN THE TWENTIETH CENTURY

By the early years of the twentieth century, weapons of war had become even more powerful and more numerous. The industrial nations, especially the major European powers, were developing long-range cannons, rapid-fire guns, bombs, and poison gas. Germany had submarines, and Great Britain developed a tank. Germany, Great Britain, and the United States had first-rate navies. Armies were better trained and dis-

Out of World War I came two twentieth century weapons of destruction: the tank and the airplane.

ciplined than in the past. And the newly invented airplane offered an awesome potential for destruction from the sky.

WORLD WAR I

When World War I broke out in Europe in 1914, the nations involved were well prepared to inflict heavy damage upon one another. In ghastly trench warfare that extended from the North Sea to Switzerland, the armies of Britain and France—and eventually those of the United States—faced Germany and its allies. The armies dug in, barbed wire went up, machine guns and artillery were put in place, and for four long years the armies pounded at each other. At the end, in 1918, more than 8 million soldiers had died.

As in earlier wars, civilians in the battle areas were driven from their homes and their land. In the cities civilians were experiencing the destructiveness of air power. Aircraft were first used to bomb civilian as well as military and industrial targets in World War I. London and the southern part of England were frequent German targets. Although most of the raids were at night, in June of 1917 fourteen German bombers raided London in daylight. More than 500 people were killed or injured. All in all, Britain suffered fifty-two enemy raids during the war, and about 2,000 English civilians died in them.

French and British bombers also struck at German cities. In one raid on the city of Karlsruhe, in Germany's industrial area, 120 civilians were killed.

In London many civilians sought shelter in the underground subway stations, as they were to do again in World War II. Another way to escape the worst effects of the raids was to leave the city. Often, on clear moonlit nights when a raid might be expected, those who could left London and camped out in the surrounding countryside.

Civilian casualties from air raids in World War I were minimal compared with the terrible slaughter on the battlefields. Early aircraft were limited both in range and in bomb-carrying ability. In fact, civilians were more apt to be injured by falling debris from antiaircraft missiles used against the attackers. However, air raids did have an adverse effect on civilian morale. The danger of sudden, often unexpected attacks, the sometimes haphazard bombings, the deafening sounds of exploding bombs and antiaircraft guns frightened and unnerved civilians. After a raid on London, for instance, absenteeism on jobs usually rose. And for a day or two following a raid, production in factories often fell below normal.

In World War I the United States was never subjected to the physical damage of battle or air raids. The United States entered the war late, in 1917, and never seriously expected to be attacked. There were incidents of sabotage by German spies, and the rather minor threat of a German invasion through Mexico.

In 1916, however, a year before the United States entered the war, President Woodrow Wilson set up the nation's first civil defense agency. Called the Council of National Defense, it consisted of several members of the Cabinet. It was their task to organize what was broadly called the nation's civil defense effort. State and local governments also set up civilian councils.

Apparently, however, their efforts were not very effective. There was no organized system for warning people in case of attack. No plans were drawn up to get people to places of safety or to build shelters. No system was developed to train people in rescue work or in the evacuation of cities in case of attack. Americans, however, did support the war effort with enthusiasm, patriotism, and national unity. Thousands of miles from Europe's battlefields, they felt secure from attack. A little over two decades later, security on the home front could not be taken so easily for granted.

WORLD WAR II

By the 1930s, Europe was heading for another war, which would eventually involve the United States and the Soviet Union—as well as Japan and China. Having seen what air power could do to cities and their civilian populations, Great Britain, France, and Germany began making preparations to defend their people. By 1938, Britain drew up civil defense plans. Air-raid warning systems were established. Rescue services, such as ambulance corps and fire-fighting teams, were organized throughout Great Britain at the local level. Plans were made to evacuate the cities and transport people—especially children—to the relative safety of the countryside. Thousands of volunteers were being trained to act as air-raid wardens.

When war came in 1939, Great Britain put its plans into action. At the approach of enemy planes, sirens sounded and civilians took to the shelters. Most of these were underground areas in public buildings or subway stations, and volunteer air-raid wardens directed and guided people. Many others in the outlying districts of cities simply went to their basements. At first the public shelters were crowded, badly ventilated, and lacked adequate lighting. Gradually, however, many of them were improved. Medical facilities were installed, water was supplied, and bunks were set up for people to sleep in. As the raids over London and other cities increased, people routinely entered the shelters even before the alarm sounded.

At night, throughout Great Britain, all public lights were turned off, and people drew the curtains in their homes in an attempt to avoid presenting easily visible targets to enemy aircraft. Places of business were darkened, too. One of the tasks of air-raid wardens was to make sure that in their areas the blackout was strictly enforced.

Airplane-spotting stations were set up all along the eastern coast of Great Britain. As soon as enemy planes were seen, the warning went out. Since spotters could not predict exactly where the planes were heading, cities usually got about a fifteen- or twenty-minute warning. For those who didn't want to go to the shelters—and no one was forced to—the rule was simply "duck and cover."

British cities suffered terrible damage from enemy raids in World War II. Coventry was nearly reduced to rubble; central London lost a fourth of its buildings. It has been said that without the heroic and determined efforts of Britain's civil defense force, Great Britain might well have been forced to surrender. In addition, the morale of British civilians remained high. One

In this 1940 photograph, civilians in London, England, are shown catching up on their sleep in the comparative safety of a subway station converted into an air raid shelter.

reason was the work of well-trained air-raid wardens. They were usually assigned to their own neighborhoods, where the people knew and respected them.

When the United States entered World War II in December 1941, it was not nearly as well prepared to protect its civilians. The United States had tried to maintain its neutrality; however, a draft was implemented to increase the size of the armed forces, and industries such as steel, rubber, automobile manufacturing, and shipbuilding began to shift to the production of war matériel. In the spring of 1941, the Office of Civil Defense (OCD) was established. The mayor of New York, Fiorello La Guardia, was appointed to head it. Charged with organizing volunteers in all the cities and towns of the nation to protect civilians in case of air raids, La Guardia was to set up a network of air-raid wardens and shelters. His office was also supposed to encourage people to conserve food and collect scrap metal for the war effort and, in general, boost civilian morale.

In addition, in early 1941, cities around the nation began to organize their own civil defense programs. Volunteer fire brigades were formed. Thousands of people attended classes in first aid and survival techniques, and thousands more registered as air-raid wardens. In New York City, 60,000 people signed up in the summer of 1941. The government also began to establish a volunteer aircraft spotting network to track hostile aircraft in time of war. This network was modeled on the British system, and it became known as the Civilian Air Warning System.

By the time of the Japanese attack on Pearl Harbor in December 1941, around a million volunteers were enrolled in the local chapters of the OCD. But these chapters were poorly organized and rather inept. Many communities were dissatisfied with their efforts, refused to cooperate with "La Guardia's volunteers," and set up their own civil defense. When the local authorities tried to take over from the OCD chapters, the result was often a great deal of confusion. False alarms threw some cities into panic. At the report of Japanese planes overhead, air-raid sirens sounded in San Francisco the day after the United States declared war on Japan. In Los Angeles an imaginary air raid brought out antiaircraft guns that blazed away into the darkness. Scores of civilians were injured by falling shrapnel before it was realized that there was no raid. On the East Coast, people prepared to evacuate their children, and state and local authorities levied stiff fines and sometimes jail sentences for anyone who disobeyed the orders of an air-raid warden.

Eventually, however, the civil defense efforts became organized. By the summer of 1942, about 11,000 local defense councils were in operation, with nearly ten million volunteers. Air-raid alarm systems were set up, and emergency shelters were designated. Blackouts were common, especially practice blackout "emergencies." Sirens would sound, and the aircraft spotters would assume their stations. Emergency shelters were readied and ambulances were called out. A warning signal sounded the approach of enemy planes, all traffic was stopped, and all public lighting was turned off. Searchlights beamed on, while United States Army planes flew overhead. Soon civil defense headquarters would begin to receive reports of buildings bombed, railway stations blown up, and hundreds of civilian casualties. Air-raid rescue workers and ambulances rushed to the scene. These practice emergencies were fairly popular with the public and also highlighted the importance of civil defense.

In addition, thousands of civilian pilots joined the Civil Air Patrol. They watched for enemy submarines in coastal waters and carried high-priority materials, such as medicines or official documents, from place to place. They were soon joined by thousands of small-boat owners who also took part in antisubmarine watches.

The Office of Civil Defense had problems throughout its existence, with shortages of equipment for fire fighting and rescue work. The agency also had trouble from time to time with uncooperative local officials. When it became clear that the United States was not going to be attacked directly, operations such as the practice blackouts ceased, and coastal patrols were disbanded. When that happened, the Office of Civil Defense concentrated on coordinating the nation's overall civilian volunteer efforts to support the war. The OCD was never as important as the government agencies that coordinated the labor, agricultural, and industrial efforts of the nation during the war. Nevertheless, it showed that the United States was serious about civil defense, and it set the precedent for future civil defense programs.

THE NUCLEAR AGE ARRIVES

The world was never the same after August 6, 1945, the day a U.S. B-29 dropped an atomic bomb on Hiroshima, Japan. Within seconds, 71,000 people were killed; many more died later of injuries and radiation effects. The city was destroyed.

The United States now had the power to kill tens of thousands of people with one bomb. Five years later, the Soviet Union had the same capabilities. In time, other nations, too, were to acquire the technology to produce an atomic bomb.

CIVIL DEFENSE IN THE 1950s
Along with the realization of the atomic bomb's tremendous power came a growing uneasiness on the part of the American people about their former ally, the Soviet Union. Mutual suspicion and hostility were exacerbated by the Korean War, which pitted an ally of the United States—South Korea—against an ally of the Soviet Union—North Korea—a conflict into

An Allied war correspondent looks over the acres of devastation in Hiroshima in September of 1945, one month after an atomic bomb destroyed the city.

which the United States was eventually drawn. (The Korean War lasted from 1950 to 1953 and would probably have gone on longer had it not been for newly elected President Dwight Eisenhower's avowal that he would use atomic weapons if necessary to bring the war to an end.)

A few months after the first Soviet atomic bomb was tested, a congressional committee on atomic energy held hearings on civil defense. The National Security Council recommended that the government set up defenses against air attack, and as a result, the Federal Civil Defense Administration (FCDA) was established, under the jurisdiction of the White House.

The primary responsibility for civil defense was in the hands of state and local officials, with assistance from the FCDA, which was authorized to train officials, develop standards for shelters, and organize emergency warning and communications systems.

The FCDA was also authorized to give funds to state civil defense programs, but as early as President Harry Truman's administration, the White House learned that it would not be so easy to get Congress to vote approval of money for civil defense. Referring to civil defense in his 1951 budget request, President Truman said, "I want to be as clear about this as I can. We simply cannot afford a penny-wise pound-foolish attitude about the cost of adequate civil defense. Everyone in this country—all of us—must face the fact that civil defense is, and will continue to be just as vital to American security as our armed forces, our defense production, and our aid to allies and friends abroad."

Harry Truman may not have wanted to be penny-wise and pound-foolish. But apparently Congress did. Once Congress had created the FCDA, it refused to give the agency the massive funding it requested. It began by rejecting the agency's request for an $11 billion, five-year program.

In fact, over the years civil defense has not been very heavily funded by Congress, compared with appropriations for military defense and offense. The disparity between what a president requests and what is actually given is very often vast. In 1951 President Truman requested about $400 million; he got $75 million. In 1952, the same year the United States tested its first hydrogen bomb, the budget request soared to $600 million. Congress appropriated even less than the year before—$50 million. The history of budget requests for civil defense funding during the 1950s and 1960s shows a tremendous fluctuation, while actual appropriations remained at a fairly even level.

Whether or not the federal government could or would implement a comprehensive, well-funded civil defense program, interest in civil defense at the local level was high at first. Many people began stockpiling their cellars with canned food, first-aid materials, and such tools as flashlights and shovels. Encouraging the construction of private bomb shelters, the government prepared handbooks on how to build permanent home shelters—both below ground, in a basement, and above ground, in a yard or garden. The plans for constructing home shelters were quite detailed and included the use of such materials as wood, concrete, bricks, and sand. The handbooks also gave instructions on how to stock the shelters with supplies and how to maintain them.

There was advice, too, on how to improvise a shelter in case of sudden attack. If there was little warning time, it was suggested, people should utilize the same kind of protective materials used for more permanent shelters. In addition, bookcases, dressers, tables, trunks, and cartons (to be filled with dirt) could be used as shielding materials. These could be piled on top of a table, preferably in a basement, and then people would get under the table. These materials could also be stacked to serve as "walls."

For homes with no basements, outside "trench" shelters were advised. The handbooks suggested digging an L-shaped trench about 4 feet (122 cm) deep and 3 feet (91 cm) wide, with the short side of the L serving as an entranceway. Then the instructions were to place lumber or doors on top of the trench, pile one or two feet of dirt on the lumber, and crawl in.

One thing the handbooks avoided mentioning was the cost of the more permanent shelters. One private luxury shelter was built on Long Island, New York, at a cost of $50,000—in the 1950s. The shelter could accommodate nine people for six weeks after an attack. Its walls were 2.5 feet (76 cm) thick and its ceiling was lined with lead. It boasted generators, heat, lighting, air filters, cooking facilities, and an indoor pump connected to a well. There were two main rooms, utility rooms, a decontamination room, and space for three servants. The person who built it held a few parties there but found no other use for it. It is now abandoned.

Public drills were held periodically, during which people were instructed to take refuge in hallways or basements, or to duck into the nearest public shelter, many of which displayed the yellow and black civil defense symbol. Shelters were also located in subways and tunnels. For people who lived in mining areas, the mines themselves were often designated public shelters. There were periodic drills in the schools, in which students crouched under desks or tables in simulated nuclear attacks.

In addition to government publications, books and articles were published on how to survive an atomic attack. One such book, *How to Survive an Atomic Bomb*, by Richard Gerstell (1950), set forth a number of rules. A paramount one, according to Gerstell, was that in case of attack, "Everyone must always lie down full-length on his stomach with his face buried in his arms." In a city one would do this next to the nearest building. Those who lived in the country were advised to stretch out in the nearest furrow of plowed land if no other protection was available. Gerstell also felt that the hazards of atomic radiation and fallout could be overcome. He recommended that after an attack everyone faithfully shower once a day. Should what Gerstell called "hot dust" appear in people's homes after an attack, they were advised to clean their houses from top to bottom.

One of the most important works of fiction of this era was Nevil Shute's *On the Beach,* a portrayal of the end of the world

In Cleveland, Ohio, in 1951, school children take refuge under their desks during a civil defense drill.

seen through the eyes of a submarine crew who escaped the final war by remaining submerged. The submarine roams the oceans, surfacing only to find total desolation everywhere but one spot in Australia. The crew joins the world's remaining survivors, and at the book's conclusion, they are all awaiting the radiation that will kill them. The book was made into a successful film.

In the early 1950s, fear of nuclear war led to the rise of atomic-age real estate. Newspapers in Washington, D.C., advertised homes that were "a safe 58 miles from Washington" and "small farms out beyond the range of A-bombs."

Aside from looking for "safe" homes, people also thought about ways to protect their bodies from atomic hazards. In 1951 one ingenious inventor came up with a pair of atomic-age pajamas for his young son. Made of a quilted material, the pajamas were filled with 5 pounds (2.3 kg) of shredded lead. Carrying around 5 pounds of lead would be quite a burden for an adult, let alone a child. However, the Atomic Energy Commission examined the suit and pronounced it a real possibility as protection against atomic radiation.

The survival handbooks, the how-to manuals, atomic-age clothing, and "safe" real estate may seem naive to us today, but in the 1950s people were not well informed about nuclear weapons and the terrible effects of a possible nuclear war. In fact, most people were unfamiliar with such terms as *fallout, ground zero, fission, fusion, megaton, rem, firestorm,* and *thermonuclear.*

If people were not too knowledgeable about nuclear weapons and their effects, it was partly because of government secrecy. In 1946 the Atomic Energy Act had created a classification system called Restricted Data. Much information about nuclear weapons was in this category. Material about the design, manufacture, or testing of nuclear weapons was supposed to be available only to a selected few in government and scientific circles. It was not to be readily available to the general public.

In 1950, for example, the government's decision to push forward with the development of the hydrogen bomb was made by a small group of politicians and scientists. That approach was roundly criticized by physicist Louis N. Ridenour. In an article in *Scientific American,* Ridenour denounced the decision as being made "without anything that could have been called informed public discussion. The public did not even know, and still does not, what the actual questions at issue were."

In fact, even scientists and other specialists in the atomic field often had difficulty in getting information or, more important, in giving out information about nuclear weapons. In 1950 *Scientific American* got into trouble with the Atomic Energy Commission. The physicist Hans Bethe wrote an article giving some pertinent facts about the hydrogen bomb. *Scientific American* was ready to print it when the Atomic Energy Commission stepped in, insisting on rewriting the article and deleting some of the facts. *Scientific American* charged the government with suppressing vital information that would help the public make intelligent and informed judgments about the hydrogen bomb. Bethe, the author of the article, was himself a government consultant, and he did not want to fight the commission. In the end, the magazine published a watered-down version of the article.

As further testing of the bomb proceeded, the government continued to restrict information and to present the results of testing in vague, general terms. In 1953 President Eisenhower cautioned the head of the Atomic Energy Commission to keep such terms as *thermonuclear* and *hydrogen* out of information given to the newspapers. Eisenhower also suggested that "they" be kept confused about the meaning of the words *fission* and *fusion*.

In 1954 the United States tested a fifteen-megaton hydrogen bomb in the Pacific Ocean, in the vicinity of the Marshall Islands. Fallout spread over an area of about 7,000 square miles (18,000 sq km). Some American servicemen were contaminated, along with a Japanese fishing-boat crew, one of whom died from the effects of radioactive fallout six months later. When newspaper reporters asked for a description of what had occurred, Eisenhower said the information was classified.

The general public could also expect to be confused when the experts disagreed among themselves about the effects of nuclear war. In response to the testing of the hydrogen bomb, eleven noted scientists, including Albert Einstein, issued a public statement about the dangers of radioactive fallout. "The best authorities," they said, "are unanimous in saying that a war with H-bombs might quite possibly put an end to the human race. It is feared that if many H-bombs are used there will be universal death—sudden only for a minority, but for the majority a slow torture of disease and disintegration." Nobel Prize winner Linus Pauling echoed this view, stating that each bomb that was tested could eventually cause the death of 100,000 people because of radiation effects.

While downplaying nuclear war as a catastrophe, Herman Kahn, a nuclear weapons analyst, also wrote about the effects of radioactive fallout on future generations. Kahn estimated that as a result of radioactive fallout, about 1 percent of the children born of survivors would be defective. That, he admitted, was 25 percent above the normal level. He went on to say that these defects might continue for up to forty generations. However, Kahn concluded, this was "a long way from annihilation."

In 1955 the Soviet Union tested its first hydrogen bomb. The United States, suspecting that the Soviets had embarked on a massive arms buildup, concluded that it must match these efforts. As more and more nuclear weapons were developed and tested, the thrust of civil defense changed. The idea of shelters was all but abandoned when the government realized that shelters, especially in urban areas, could not withstand the blast effects of such a powerful weapon as the hydrogen bomb. The explosive potential of this bomb was nearly unlimited. Rather than shelters, officials began to think in terms of evacuating large urban populations to "safe" areas.

Along with a belief in "crisis relocation"

as a civil defense measure came plans to preserve the government leadership in the event of a nuclear attack. Away from such a prime target as Washington, D.C., Mount Weather, a self-sufficient community, was hollowed out of a remote section of Virginia's Blue Ridge Mountains as an alternate national capital. Here, if it should become necessary, key officials could gather to wait out a nuclear attack and to assure the continuity of government.

In the presidential campaign of 1956, Democratic candidate Adlai Stevenson called for an international ban on the testing of the hydrogen bomb, warning that the atmosphere was being poisoned by radioactive fallout.

In 1957 the Soviet Union launched *Sputnik*, the world's first artificial satellite. The news of the successful launch was chilling, for it meant that nuclear warheads could someday be delivered by missiles in a matter of minutes. Soon afterward a special government panel on defense policy pressed President Eisenhower to institute a massive civil defense effort. The panel's recommendation was for a $44 billion, five-year plan. The president did not follow the panel's advice. Instead he submitted a modest budget of around $140 million, and Congress cut even that. A good share of the Eisenhower administration's reaction to *Sputnik* centered instead on efforts to get funds for more and better education in science and mathematics to better equip Americans to meet the Soviet challenge in space.

The year following the successful launching of *Sputnik*, Congress replaced the FCDA with yet another civil defense agency, the Office of Civil Defense Mobilization (OCDM). This agency had joint responsibility with state and local officials for preparing the nation to meet civil defense emergencies. The OCDM was not very effective, however. Part of this was because of public apathy and lack of knowledge. A study conducted at the time showed that half of the people questioned didn't know of anything they could do to protect themselves before a nuclear attack. Only 15 percent mentioned building shelters in their homes as one thing they could do. Another study carried out in 1959 on public awareness of civil defense in New York State concluded that, "Unfortunately the public is not yet aware of the knowledge which is basic to its survival. The average individual does not now understand the threat of radiation or how to protect against it. Nor does he know how to tell when it is present, or have any conception of how much he can receive without becoming ill." As the 1950s came to a close, it seemed that the technology of nuclear weapons was running far ahead of any civil defense methods.

CIVIL DEFENSE IN THE 1960s

In the presidential campaign of 1960, John Kennedy accused Eisenhower of not preparing the country to deal with a Soviet missile threat. Soon after his election, Kennedy gave his views on civil defense when he stated, "Civil defense can be readily justifiable as insurance for the civilian population, in case of an enemy miscalculation. It is insurance we trust will never be needed, but insurance which we could never forgive ourselves for forgoing in the event of catastrophe." Kennedy said he would ask

On October 23, 1962, President John F. Kennedy signed a proclamation formally putting into effect an arms blockade of Cuba. Many people believed we were on the brink of a nuclear war.

for funds to identify and mark fallout shelters and to stock them with food, water, and first-aid kits. Kennedy also vowed to create warning and detection systems. He was going to push for a system that included a nuclear-war alarm in every American home.

Once in office, Kennedy rearranged civil defense planning yet again. This time he made the Pentagon, under the Department of Defense, responsible for coordinating civil defense. Congress approved Kennedy's request for $207 million to implement his program.

Then, in 1961, a crisis occurred over the construction of a wall by the Communist East Germans that cut the city of Berlin in half and temporarily isolated the Western sectors, creating the kind of tension between the United States and the Soviet Union that could lead to war. The United States government began a program to identify public places that could be used as fallout shelters; these were stocked with food and medicines.

How effective would these shelters have been in the event of a nuclear attack? The government reasoned that 2 feet (61 cm) of concrete or 3 feet (91 cm) of earth was sufficient to protect against fallout, but not against a blast.

The year after the Berlin crisis came a threat much closer to home, when U.S. spy planes discovered Soviet missiles based in Cuba. President Kennedy ordered a blockade of the island, and the United States prepared for war. For eight days a pall hung over the country. People in densely populated areas, such as Washington, D.C. and

New York City, waited in resigned despair, wondering if their lives were soon to end in a moment's flash. Others were not so resigned; more than ten million Americans left the cities in preparation for nuclear war. Those along the southeast coast of Florida prepared to evacuate.

But the Soviets backed down, proving to the Americans that the United States had the military might to deter them. The Cuban missile crisis also showed that civil defense was not well planned enough to mobilize 200 million people and effectively protect them. Kennedy became convinced that civil defense as protection for the population in a nuclear war was not possible. Blast protection was not feasible, and a mass evacuation of people would require the regimentation of society.

Kennedy expressed his views in the following speech: "It [civil defense] cannot deter a nuclear attack. We will deter an enemy from making a nuclear attack only if our retaliatory power is so strong and invulnerable that he knows he would be destroyed by our response. If we have the strength, civil defense is not needed to deter an attack. If we should ever lack it, civil defense would not be an adequate substitute."

Given this attitude on the part of the government, it isn't too surprising that Congress fell back into its old habits and continued to cut presidential requests for civil defense funding.

The government may have slacked off in its civil defense efforts, but the experts continued their debate over the hazards of nuclear war and the effectiveness of civil defense. In 1963 biologist Bentley Glass estimated probable deaths in a nuclear war as about 82 percent within sixty days, and a total of about 90 percent casualties following that period, depending on the weapons used and how they were targeted over the population of a country. He went on to describe the horrors faced by the survivors. Few animal sources of food would remain, and without birds the insect population would proliferate. Cockroaches, he noted, can tolerate 40,000 rems of radiation and survive. Unless fires did a thorough job of consuming the dead, unburied corpses would litter the land, and epidemics would spread rapidly. Millions of survivors, according to Glass, would die slow deaths from hunger and disease.

On the other hand, Earl Voss, a proponent of nuclear testing also writing in 1963, scoffed at the fear of radioactive fallout. He maintained, "Natural radiation or X rays, administered by doctors, dentists, and shoe clerks, had been much more dangerous for 99 percent of the world's peoples." Voss pointed out with some logic that people were frightened by the radiation that would result from nuclear wars, but that few had given any serious thought to halting the nuclear-weapons testing, which also spread deadly fallout. Voss concluded that the fear of fallout was a result of Soviet propaganda. He felt that the Soviet Union wanted to "sow confusion [and] perhaps to persuade the West to join in outlawing the use of nuclear weapons in warfare."

A series of opinion polls in the mid-1960s found that roughly two out of three Americans favored civil defense measures.

This attitude, the polls found, had little to do with the amount of knowledge the particular persons had about civil defense. Most had little information. The polls also showed that people favored civil defense measures even though the government was not pushing a comprehensive civil defense program. As for specific programs, the polls did show that people did not want to build home shelters—unless the government paid for them. The majority of people favored protecting schools and schoolchildren. They also favored the construction of blast shelters in cities. But the experts concluded that this was because the people interviewed didn't know of the difficulties of building blast shelters in large urban areas. Many people felt that they would not survive the effects of fallout unless they had fallout shelters. The polls showed that people thought shelters were fairly effective.

Whether or not shelters were effective, many groups advocated their construction and use. In 1965 a group of scientists connected with the Lawrence Radiation Laboratory in Livermore, California, presented the results of its construction of a group fallout shelter near Livermore. The scientists had formed a corporation called Survival Associates, Inc., and recruited members.

The description of the shelter is detailed and in some instances rather technical. Basically it was designed to hold about thirty-five families, or about 100 people. Each family was assigned a section, which included a family room about 7.5 feet (2.3 m) square, a kitchen, and toilet facilities.

Water was stored in huge tanks buried beneath the floor of the shelter. Lighting was fluorescent and could be powered by generators in case nearby utilities were knocked out by a nuclear attack. Air was drawn into the shelter through specially located intake pipes. Knowledgeable about the patterns of radioactive fallout (gathered from the results of nuclear testing), the scientists had devised a ventilation system that would let in the least amount of contaminated air.

The overall shelter was a steel arch covered with earth. The floor was a concrete slab six inches (15 cm) thick, which was reinforced with steel. The walls were reinforced with steel rods to keep them from collapsing inward. The corporation claimed that the shelter could withstand a 20 psi (pounds per square inch) overpressure without too much damage. The shelter was surrounded by an 8-foot-high (2-m) chain link fence topped with barbed wire.

The kinds of food stored in the shelter included dried and canned goods. The food chosen had to have a fairly long shelf life so that it would not have to be replaced too often. First-aid supplies were also included, but there were no arrangements for any serious medical emergencies.

The corporation also conducted some occupancy tests. In three tests, twenty-five people occupied the shelter for twelve hours. They stayed overnight and prepared breakfast using the facilities of the shelter. In a fourth test, ninety-five people stayed in the shelter for thirty-eight hours. These tests were to show how the shelter could meet the needs of people in an emergency and to see how people reacted. According to the corporation's report, the ventilation system worked well, even when closed off for four hours to monitor the amounts of oxygen and other gases in the air. The people had no objections to the canned and dried foods, and managed to cope with the kitchen and sanitation facilities. Of course, they were only in the shelter for several hours. In a nuclear attack, they might have to occupy the place for weeks at a time.

The cost of this group shelter, including the operating expenses, was nearly $68,000. The cost per family came to about $2,000. The corporation also carried fire insurance. This cost was high because there was no adequate water supply nearby, the local fire-fighting services were minimal, and the steel shell of the building was considered likely to collapse from a fire inside. It does seem curious that the structure was expected to withstand a tremendous amount of blast pressure, was supposed to minimize the effects of fallout, was said to be habitable for lengthy periods of time, and yet was not considered a very good insurance risk.

The construction and operation of this group shelter were based on the theory that there would be no surprise attack on the United States. Survival Associates believed that before any attack, there would be a period of crisis during which people would have plenty of time to reach the shelter and get it into operating condition. The members of the corporation did concede that in a surprise attack with multiple use of nuclear weapons, people would have difficulty surviving.

By the mid-1960s, shelter construction companies had pretty much disappeared. People might still fear the terrible results of a nuclear war, but the *threat* of such a war seemed to be diminishing.

Civil defense in the United States is a history of starts and stops. In a period of crisis, tensions mount and there is a flurry of civil defense activity. When the crisis eases, efforts at civil defense diminish.

In 1963 the United States, the Soviet Union, and Great Britain signed a nuclear test-ban treaty. The pact banned tests in the air, in outer space, and in the oceans—but not underground. This seemed to be a step forward in controlling nuclear weapons. In 1967 the United States and the Soviet Union, along with sixty-one other nations, signed a pact to ban the orbiting of nuclear weapons in space.

In spite of these efforts at control, however, the arms race between the United States and the Soviet Union went on at an alarming rate. Both nations were rapidly building arsenals of missiles, submarines, and bombers. Both nations also began to put their missiles in underground silos and on submarines to make sure these weapons would be available if one nation was forced to retaliate against the other. By the end of the 1960s, the two superpowers were at a standoff. Each was capable of destroying the other several times over. This policy was called mutual assured destruction, or MAD, the idea being that neither side would use its massive arsenal because all-out nuclear war was suicidal.

Still, the intensity of the arms race did concern officials on both sides. In 1969 the United States and the Soviet Union began negotiations to try to limit strategic weapons. Strategic weapons are those designed to destroy a nation's overall military might. They include long-range missiles based on land, long-range bombers, and missiles based on submarines. Negotiations for the treaty continued until 1972.

A massive arms buildup accompanied by a falling off of civil defense efforts seems contradictory. But two beliefs were widely held at the time: first, that the policy of mutual assured destruction would prevent a war, and second, if a war occurred, civil defense measures would be useless anyway. As the 1970s approached, an era of détente, or easing of tensions between the superpowers, was beginning.

CIVIL DEFENSE IN THE 1970s

In 1972, a five-year Strategic Arms Limitation Treaty (SALT I) was concluded between the United States and the Soviet Union, imposing limits on antiballistic missile systems (ABMs). ABMs are defensive weapons designed to destroy an enemy's incoming missiles. The treaty limited each nation to two ABM sites. One U.S. site was to be around Washington, D.C., and one Soviet site around Moscow. The United States did explore the possibility of putting one site near Grand Forks, North Dakota. But the people there objected, and the project was eventually scrapped.

SALT I also put some limitations on offensive weapons and set the stage for further negotiations to conclude a SALT II treaty. During the SALT I talks, American negotiators put forth the idea that both sides should abandon their plans for sheltering their populations, but nothing came of the proposal.

The idea behind the limitation of ABMs was to reinforce the doctrine that defense against nuclear weapons was impossible. It was thought that having a defensive missile system would make a nation feel secure against attack. Feeling secure, a nation might not want to enter into negotiations to halt the spread of nuclear weapons.

With SALT I and the era of détente, civil defense plans were curtailed. Budget requests and appropriations declined sharply; remaining shelters were abandoned, and stored food and medicines rotted. However, some experts cautioned that while the United States was neglecting civil defense, the Soviet Union was building up its own civil defense program. While some thought the Soviet buildup was simply because that nation was traditionally suspicious of Western intentions, others believed differently. These analysts thought the Soviet Union was preparing for a nuclear war it thought it could win.

Under the administrations of Presidents Richard Nixon and Gerald Ford, negotiations for a SALT II treaty continued. At the same time, defense planners began to think in terms of a "limited" nuclear war. In 1974 Secretary of Defense James R. Schlesinger announced that the United States was going to develop long-range nuclear missiles of great accuracy, weapons capable of hitting very specific targets, both industrial and military. And since the weapons would be so accurate, they would not have to be as large as previous weapons to be effective against such enemy weapons as land-based missiles. (The Soviet Union had more land-based missiles than the United States.) Coupled with the idea of a limited nuclear war was an emphasis by military planners on a stepped-up program of civil defense.

President Jimmy Carter came into office in 1977. He continued negotiations for a SALT II treaty, even though the prospects of coming to an agreement with the Soviet Union over limiting nuclear weapons now seemed dim. At the same time some defense experts warned that a civil defense gap was developing between the United States and the Soviet Union.

Apparently, however, these warnings had little effect on civil defense planning by the government. Even after two years in office, the Carter administration had no coherent civil defense strategy. Shelters in major cities and other areas that could be enemy targets were not blastproof and were therefore useless (although critics of shelters argue that there is no such thing as a blastproof shelter). Food and medical stockpiles had deteriorated. No overall plan for evacuating cities had been formulated. There were no plans to feed, house, or treat injured evacuees.

President Jimmy Carter is shown holding hands with Soviet President Leonid Brezhnev in Vienna, Austria, in 1979, during negotiations for the SALT II treaty.

In 1978 the Pentagon estimated that a civil defense program comparable to the Soviet system would cost from $20 to $40 billion. It also concluded that such an amount would be better spent on weapons. At the same time the Arms Control and Disarmament Agency released a report of American and Soviet capabilities through the mid-1980s. It concluded that the United States led the Soviet Union in its ability to destroy targets. It also stated that by the mid-1980s both nations would have essentially equal capabilities. A Pentagon official pointed out, too, that if a civil defense gap should occur, the United States could reverse its policy of only targeting military and industrial areas and target civilian populations.

Some experts in the Carter administration thought the best way to handle civil defense was to neglect the whole issue. One administration official said: "The only realistic danger lies in the exaggeration of Soviet civil defense and the American response to it . . . the more attention we pay to it, the more tensions rise, making war more likely, not less."

In 1978 President Carter authorized the consolidation of most government organizations responsible for civil defense into an independent agency—the Federal Emergency Management Agency (FEMA). Carter's directive provided for the evacuation of cities and the relocation of people as the nation's principal method of civil defense. Carter did not, however, ask Congress to increase civil defense funding. During his presidency, funding stayed at about $100 million a year.

In his last year in office, Carter issued other presidential directives concerning civil defense. One directive gave a higher priority to attacking Soviet military targets in case of war. It also emphasized destroying the Soviet Union's top leaders. Another directive provided measures to ensure governmental continuity in the United States following a nuclear attack.

Critics of Carter's directives claimed they indicated the government was heading toward acceptance of limited nuclear war. They argued that officials seemed to be thinking more and more that a nuclear war could be limited to acceptable levels of damage, and was in fact "winnable." That is, the warring nation that emerged with the least devastation would have won.

However, Carter's civil defense policies were not much different from those of his predecessors, except that the evacuation of civilians and their relocation outside cities became the basic plan for protecting the populace; this was picked up and embellished by the following administration.

CIVIL DEFENSE IN THE 1980s

In March 1982 President Ronald Reagan disclosed plans for a seven-year civil defense program that was estimated to cost $4.2 billion—the largest civil defense budget ever proposed. The director of FEMA, Louis O. Giuffrida, told a House of Representatives subcommittee: "Although previous administrations have talked about civil defense, none have applied the necessary money and effort. President Reagan," he added, "means to get the job done."

President Reagan directed FEMA to think in terms of three key elements in case of nuclear war: population protection, industrial protection, and blast shelters. The president's directive stated the hope that by the end of 1989, plans would be completed to move the populations of large urban areas, or high-risk areas, to surrounding areas of lower risk. This would be done, the directive stated, using the "extensive U.S. transportation resources." The president also directed that efforts be made to protect key industrial and defense workers. He asked that money be made available to build blast shelters for these people so that they could carry on their work.

To implement the president's directive, much of the federal money would go to state and local governments. They would be responsible for local planning to evacuate the cities and relocate people in safer areas. Some funds would go for upgrading communications systems nationwide to lessen their vulnerability to attack. Other money would go to increasing the survival chances of key federal officials.

FEMA estimates that even with the program, millions of lives would still be lost. However, says the agency, 80 percent of the population would survive, compared with 20 to 40 percent if a nuclear attack were to occur today. According to FEMA's projected procedure, after it has been ascertained that the Soviet Union is going to attack, a warning will be sounded and people will take preplanned action to leave the cities. More than two million "emergency managers," most of them police, firefighters, and other local officials, will put FEMA's evacuation plan into effect. When people get to areas outside the cities, sturdy basements, buildings, and even foxhole "expedient" shelters will be available to them. Food and other supplies will be waiting.

Even with this plan, a FEMA spokesman admitted that "your problems are still catastrophic, but at least they are more manageable—and more people will live." Director Giuffrida told a House subcommittee about the warning time needed. "Even if we have as little as three hours' warning, our program will save lives. If we have a week's warning, our program will be of significant benefit."

FEMA's plans aroused a storm of controversy. Opposition came from communities across the country. Some communities voted not to cooperate in any way with federal civil defense planners. Harold Brown, former President Carter's secretary of defense, declared that the massive buildup was unjustified. Senator Alan Cranston of California stated: "Study after study has shown that it is a cruel delusion to believe that civil defense offers meaningful security against all-out nuclear attack." In an editorial, *The New York Times* soundly criticized the proposals "People who think that even with a week's warning they could evacuate two-thirds of the American people, feed them for a month in remote fallout shelters and then resume life in 300 or more devastated cities ought themselves to be evacuated from government forthwith."

If nothing else, the cost of the program will be a stumbling block to its success. Congress has, as noted, never been generous with civil defense funds. During a time of mounting federal deficits and cutbacks in all kinds of programs, it is unlikely that Congress will vote massive amounts of money for civil defense. How FEMA will continue its programs and implement its plans for a comprehensive, nationwide system remains to be seen.

ON THE DRAWING BOARD— CIVIL DEFENSE AT HOME AND ABROAD

In case of a nuclear attack, one of the primary concerns of the Federal Emergency Management Agency would be to protect civilians. Because of the mobility of the American population, FEMA places more emphasis on evacuating civilians from urban centers than on constructing shelters. "Crisis relocation" is the removal of civilians from so-called risk areas to so-called host communities. Risk areas are cities with populations of more than 50,000. There are also counterforce areas of risk—those that have strategic offensive forces, such as missiles, submarines, and manned bombers.

Host communities are those that would be located at least 20 miles (32 km) from military installations, industrial sites, and other likely targets of an enemy attack. The host communities would be prepared to receive the evacuees. Various types of shelters would be stocked with provisions.

The success of crisis relocation rests on the premise that there would be adequate warning of an impending attack. Telltale signs, such as the evacuation of Moscow and other Soviet cities, would be observed by satellite and reported immediately. A warning network would be activated and emergency evacuation plans put into effect.

During 1982, FEMA completed around 1,000 plans pertaining to crisis relocation nationwide. About 3,000 plans in all are expected to be prepared. The completed plans cover 36 million risk-area residents. FEMA also completed about 70 percent of its plans for dealing with residents in the counterforce high-risk areas. In addition nearly 159,000 buildings were surveyed in 1982 for crisis-relocation purposes.

FEMA is also in charge of stockpiling materials such as food and medical supplies for use in case of war. For instance, in 1980, the agency had 70,000 pounds of morphine stored to use to treat victims of a possible war. Although it wanted to purchase about 10,000 more pounds, the Reagan administration decided to defer the purchase on the grounds that it might appear to the public as if the United States was preparing to engage in a limited nuclear war. Some officials felt the purchase would be useless anyway, since there were no good plans in place to distribute the drug.

FEMA puts out a comprehensive catalog of its numerous publications. These range from handbooks for the general public to instruction manuals for people in local civil defense. Most of these publications concern planning, training, and management in case of natural disasters. Some, however, offer instructions for the general public on how to build home fallout shelters. Most of these are dated 1980. Although FEMA is concentrating its efforts on its crisis-relocation plans, it still has not entirely abandoned the idea that fallout shelters can be effective, as well as useful. Describing outside, underground shelters, one handbook notes that the roof of the shelter "can be used as an attractive patio." And an aboveground shelter could be used as a toolshed or workshop. Another handbook suggests building a basement snack bar of brick and concrete, which can then be converted into an inside shelter.

FEMA stresses the importance of state and local governments in developing programs and plans for the safety of their people, and will assist by providing money and training for civil defense personnel. It also gives guidance and advice to private groups that want to develop civil defense plans. Most of FEMA's work with local communities, however, relates to natural disasters. For instance, if a tornado strikes an area, FEMA sets up a Disaster Assistance Center to offer aid to affected communities. FEMA may help provide temporary housing or provide low-interest loans to people or businesses to help them recover. It can also give grants-in-aid to state and local governments. In the meantime FEMA continues to develop its programs and plans for crisis relocation in case of nuclear attack.

CIVIL DEFENSE IN THE SOVIET UNION Information on the civil defense system of the Soviet Union has been compiled mostly by U.S. government agencies, particularly the defense and intelligence agencies, and generally comes from two kinds of sources—"open" and "closed." Open sources are books, newspapers, and maga-

In this 1962 photograph supplied to Western reporters by the Soviet government, a guide points out features of a shelter model displayed at a civil defense exhibition in Moscow.

zines from the Soviet Union that are available either in Russian or in translation. Closed sources are those whose information has been obtained by secret or sensitive methods. For national security reasons, these closed sources are not revealed to the general public.

One of the most comprehensive reports on Soviet civil defense is a 1978 study compiled by the U.S. Central Intelligence Agency (CIA). The study includes information gathered from both open and closed sources, and is used by U.S. military and civil defense authorities and by others who want to explore Soviet civil defense strategy. However, not everyone agrees with the study's assessments and conclusions about Soviet civil defense.

Because it has been so open to invasion, first czarist Russia and then the Soviet Union have emphasized the defense of the Russian homeland. Following the devastation of World War II, the Soviets concentrated on rebuilding their shattered economy and strengthening their military capabilities. They constructed their first atomic bomb in the late 1940s, and since then have built an enormous arsenal of nuclear and conventional weapons.

According to the CIA study, the Soviet Union began in the 1960s to increase the pace of its civil defense efforts and to integrate its civil defense system more closely with its overall military strategy. Soviet civil defense has several objectives. First is the protection of its people—the leadership, the essential work force, and the general public. Of primary importance also are the protection of the nation's economic resources and the continuation of economic activity in wartime. Soviet plans include restoring production after a nuclear attack and measures to help its surviving population recover.

Soviet civil defense is a highly structured program that has been under military control since the early 1970s. To accomplish its first objective, the protection of its people, the Soviet government has built blast shelters, established relocation sites, and developed evacuation plans. The Soviet Union is also concerned with protecting its economic structure. According to the 1978 CIA study, the emphasis in this area is directed toward protecting the work force. In another phase of their civil defense planning, easing the consequences of an enemy attack, the Soviets are training a large number of civilians in such postattack operations as first aid, clearing rubble, decontamination, and providing emergency repairs.

Soviet civil defense is staffed full-time at all levels of the government. However, in addition to an estimated 100,000 full-time civil defense employees, there are military and civilian units that play an auxiliary role, bringing the total estimated number of people involved to sixteen million.

The CIA study points up extensive shelter construction for Soviet leadership. ("Leadership" refers not just to the top government officials, but includes some 110,000 people at all levels of Soviet government and industry.) Shelters consist of strengthened command posts near Moscow and other cities and at relocation sites outside cities. Other shelters and relocation sites exist for local leaders and for those near major industrial plants. It is assumed that these shelters are stockpiled with food, medicine, and protective equipment.

Soviet civil defense plans also call for moving the populace from urban target areas. The Soviets may have more than 15,000 blast shelters that can protect 10 to 20 million people. This is about 10 to 20 percent of the population in cities of more than 100,000 people. Soviet urban dwellers could also be sheltered in subway tunnels and stations. The CIA study estimates that 75 to 90 percent of the Soviet urban population would be fairly adequately protected by the urban blast shelters.

Like planners in the United States, Soviet civil defense people anticipate that before an attack there would be a period of tension and crisis that would give them time to set their evacuation plans in motion. People would be informed of an impending attack and then moved to preassigned locations to be transported by rail or bus (or in some cases, according to the CIA study, by walking) to relocation sites. While the Soviets have blast shelters in place, they have not upgraded their fallout shelters to any great extent.

The CIA study estimates Soviet civil defense expenditures at $2 billion annually. This figure is an approximation because the costs of all elements of Soviet civil defense are not yet calculated.

In Cold War politics the Soviet policy is to play down its civil defense efforts and to accuse the United States of war fever whenever an American civil defense build-up is announced. A radio broadcast on civil defense in 1981 stated, "The role and tasks of civil defense have immensely increased in the present complicated political atmosphere, due to aggressive imperialist circles led by the USA."

At the same time Soviet radio broadcasts were alerting people to the importance of civil defense in protecting themselves from the weapons of the 1980s. A "mass defense month" was held in the western part of the Soviet Union, in the Ukraine. It focused on the condition of shelters in the area and the proper method of storing materials such as food and medicines.

More recently there have been civil defense displays and classes held on farms and in factories in the Baltic provinces of Lithuania and Estonia. People are instructed about the proper protective clothing. One radio report said, "Clothing made of synthetic and rubberized fabric, rubber footwear, and gloves have the best protective qualities." The report went on to say, "In order to increase the protective properties of everyday clothing, it must be subjected to additional sealing [by fastening] tightly."

Western civil defense analysts were probably also interested in radio reports that claimed that "new housing is being equipped, as required, with protective structures," and that in factory areas prime attention was being paid to shelters and "most important, whether establishments are capable of continuing regular production in an emergency."

COMPARING AMERICAN AND SOVIET CIVIL DEFENSE

In comparing the civil defense systems of the United States and the Soviet Union, one has to keep in mind that analyses of Soviet planning—as well as that of the United States—are open to interpretation and criticism. For instance, opponents of a massive U.S. buildup in civil defense do not necessarily accept the assessments of American or Soviet capability, whether from official or private sources. Proponents of civil defense are more apt to accept Soviet readiness and to urge a strong American civil defense effort as part of strategic planning in the event of war.

Most civil defense authorities concede that the Soviet Union is more advanced in civil defense planning than the United States. American civil defense has experienced ups and downs since World War II, and not until recently has it been considered an integral part of U.S. strategic plans. In the Soviet Union civil defense has proceeded at a fairly steady pace. The Russians may even be stepping up their efforts. According to some authorities, the Soviet Union is also thinking in terms of a nuclear war as survivable, which is a departure from the deterrence concept of mutual assured destruction.

According to the CIA report, the Soviet Union spends much more on civil defense than does the United States. Even if FEMA were to get the billions it has requested, the Soviets could no doubt spend even more. Over the years the United States has not allocated massive funds for civil defense compared with the funding for other programs, and congressional resistance to FEMA's budget request of $4.2 billion is strong. One senator called it a "dangerous waste of money."

The Soviet Union has an organized, structured network of thousands of civil defense workers at all levels of government and industry, and is capable of mobilizing many more. At this point the United

States has fewer than 10,000 full- or part-time civil defense personnel.

The public's attitudes also play an influential role in civil defense, especially in the United States. Here, attitudes have ranged from apathy or indifference to heated debates on the direction civil defense planning should take, and on whether there should be any civil defense at all that involves preparations for a nuclear war. Some public indifference may stem from the idea that "it can't happen here." Some may be the result of a lack of information. There is, in fact, information available about plans, programs, and general emergency measures of civil defense. But these mostly involve peacetime disasters and concern only one area at a time. Information about the civil defense capabilities of the entire nation is not disseminated through the media. When it is, it is surrounded by controversy. The issue of civil defense has been debated in military, scientific, and government circles since the 1950s. But grass-roots involvement is fairly recent and has grown out of the concern over nuclear war.

Not a lot is known about the attitude of the Soviet populace toward civil defense. Some studies indicate that there is a certain amount of apathy. Writing about Soviet civil defense in the *Bulletin of Atomic Scientists* in March of 1978, Fred M. Kaplan reported that many Russians treat civil defense as a joke. Kaplan said that Russians often abbreviate the phrase for civil defense to *grob*, which means "coffin." There are also reports of complaints in Soviet publications about apathetic administrators and poor civil defense planning.

However, in view of the reports that the Soviet Union is disseminating information through radio broadcasts and special campaigns, the Russian public may be better informed about civil defense than Americans.

Whether or not the Soviet Union has an advantage over the United States in its provisions for protection of its industries is not truly known. It is known that the Soviets have provided shelters and relocation sites for key people in industry, and some new industrial plants have been built away from urban centers. Intelligence sources have also found a gigantic factory hidden under a mountain east of Moscow. Intelligence sources also assume that the Soviets are "hardening" (strengthening) their industries as they are known to harden their military facilities. Several underground facilities that have been located seem to be designed to shelter machinery. Certain information on the protection of Soviet industry gathered by U.S. intelligence sources is no doubt secret and not available to the public. However, the true extent of Soviet efforts to harden their industries is still mostly a matter of assumption and conjecture.

In the United States, industry is still seen as vulnerable to a nuclear attack. In 1981 a FEMA official noted, "If American manufacturers wait for the federal government to take the lead in developing programs to protect our industrial installations, they may have to wait quite awhile."

Nevertheless, industry itself is making some efforts for its own protection, at least for the protection of its records and communications systems. AT&T's National

Emergency Control Center is buried 40 feet (12 m) underground in a rural area of New Jersey. The three-story building, girded with steel and reinforced concrete, was hacked out of granite, and includes living quarters, a control room, and a computer with AT&T's entire data system stored in it.

Some companies have people on their payrolls to help train and prepare their staffs in case of an emergency. Others already have emergency programs for their employees, and also issue updated manuals outlining procedures in first aid, fire control, and rescue techniques. Many companies, with the encouragement of civil defense planners, are establishing underground facilities for storage. Civil defense planners hope these companies will eventually use such storage facilities as protective shelters for employees and equipment in case of nuclear war.

One American company, Boeing Aerospace, did conduct a test involving the protection of machinery. They took their directions and procedures from a Soviet manual. According to the Soviet method, heavy machinery would first be packed in some crushable material and then covered with 6 feet (183 cm) of dirt. The people at Boeing calculated the number of people and hours it would take to pack and cover a very large machine used in making airplane parts. The conclusion was that all essential parts of the machine could be covered in forty-eight hours, including the time taken to get the necessary dirt. Then Boeing packed some trial objects and covered them with dirt. A conventional explosion equal to a one-megaton blast was set off 2,000 feet (610 m) away. The objects emerged still usable and with only minor damage. Boeing analysts claim the method can work on a much larger scale.

It is not certain who may have the advantage in protection of its essential leadership in case of nuclear attack. There are approximately seventy-five underground facilities around Moscow. Bunkers for the top government officials are claimed to be enclosed in large steel spheres. But for the top leadership both in the Soviet Union and the United States, the plans are cloaked in secrecy. And, in the United States at least, they are modified from year to year.

Generally it is thought that the president and other top government officials would go underground or take to the air in an attack. In the 1950s huge underground facilities were built in Virginia (Mount Weather) and Maryland, both about fifty miles from Washington. And at Andrews Air Force Base, near Washington, four Boeing 747 jumbo jets are reported to be prepared to serve as national emergency airborne command posts in the event of a nuclear war.

The bunkers outside Washington are now vulnerable to direct attack because of advances in Soviet missile technology. But even if an enemy failed to destroy the bunkers, it is not certain whether the president would have time to get to the shelters. Should the Soviets launch an attack from a submarine off the east coast of the United States, the warning time would be twelve minutes or less. Government leaders might not even have time to get to the Air Force base.

According to the Constitution, the president has fifteen possible successors after the vice president. In order to keep track of these people, and the president, a central locator system has been set up to monitor their whereabouts at all times. Current civil defense plans also provide for the protection of top members of Congress and key people in the judiciary and the Federal Reserve banks.

Both the governments of the United States and the Soviet Union emphasize the importance of evacuation of their urban populations prior to a nuclear attack. The plans of both nations are based on the premise that there will be ample warning time to put their plans into effect. Despite minimal planning at present, most civil defense experts feel the United States has an advantage in this area over the Soviet Union.

For one thing, the U.S. transportation network is much more developed than the Soviet Union's. A recent study by the Arms Control and Disarmament Agency points out that the United States has an extensive road system and a good food- and fuel-distribution system. There is plentiful housing in many rural areas. Good hotels and motels exist along the major highways. The report noted that "50 million Americans go out of town every weekend."

In the United States there is a car for every two people. Those who live in cities could use their cars to leave, carrying tools and supplies necessary for survival in the countryside, at least for a while. Cars can also be used as primitive fallout shelters if covered with dirt. Many Americans live in suburbs, which are close to main highways.

And except for centers of concentrated urban populations, most Americans could find a spot to dig a fallout shelter, providing they had the tools and the time.

A study done by the Stanford Research Institute found that an adequate evacuation plan could evacuate Philadelphia, Washington, and Boston in three days, and New York City in four. Another study commissioned by FEMA shows that 80 percent of the population of Ohio could survive with a crisis-relocation plan compared with only 20 percent without one.

In the Soviet Union, the transportation system is vulnerable. The country's highway system is underdeveloped, and much of its rail system is antiquated. Around urban areas mass transit is the chief means of getting about, and most of that is in European Russia. The number of buses, cars, and trucks is not considered adequate to handle millions of city dwellers. In addition, the majority of Soviet citizens do not have cars. As the CIA study pointed out, if it became necessary to evacuate the cities, a great many people would have to walk.

Most Soviet urban residents live in apartment houses. They lack the kinds of tools necessary to build primitive shelters once in the countryside. Some have country homes or even garden plots in the countryside, but Soviet civil defense manuals do not encourage people to try to get to them.

Once in the countryside, it would be difficult for Russians to dig their own shelters. The ground is frozen all winter long and is often muddy and soggy in the spring and summer. However, the fallout shelters that have been built in the countryside are reported to be simple and well designed. In 1978 a team of American engineers tested some of the Soviet designs and found them to be effective.

In preparing for the long-term survival of those who escape the initial blast and fallout, neither side may have much advantage. The Soviet Union has the largest land area of any nation in the world. Presumably food, medicines, fuel, and other materials essential for survival could be stored around the nation. There are reports of scores of new underground silos full of grain; supposedly these are replenished regularly to prevent spoilage. One expert points out, however, that this would barely feed 1 percent of the population within 50 miles (81 km) of them. In addition, the Soviet Union has a chronic food shortage, even in peacetime. In the event of a large-scale attack, such a shortage would lead to disaster.

The distribution of supplies necessary for survival and recovery after an attack is also a critical problem in the Soviet Union. Here the nation's vastness is a handicap. The Soviet Union has problems with transportation and distribution even in peacetime. A nuclear attack could disrupt this system almost beyond repair.

The United States has a good transportation and distribution system for food and other supplies. While not much has been done to protect this system from a nuclear attack, the United States does have a lot of experience in dealing with natural disasters. Many people in communities across the nation are trained in how to conduct evacuations, set up tent cities, and handle emergency communications. More than

25,000 natural disasters occur in the United States yearly, and for the most part people who have been trained deal with the crises smoothly. Civil defense on a local volunteer level in peacetime emergencies is still a strong force in this country. But some experts question how this would work if all the major cities were attacked and most of the resources were in a shambles.

There are still public fallout shelters across the nation, but they are no longer maintained. Their supplies have been removed or have spoiled. People no longer build private shelters, and there are no large shelter exercises. Some groups, however, have become interested in the Soviet-style fallout shelter built in the countryside. These are simple shelters dug into the ground, with walls and a roof of poles covered with plastic. The whole thing is then covered with dirt. Tested in 1978 in an Arizona desert, it appeared that one of these could withstand severe blast pressure when it survived the effects of an explosion equal to 100 tons of TNT that was set off nearby. So far, however, FEMA has shown little interest in such shelters, beyond publishing some copies of a survival handbook in which there are directions for building them.

As in earlier decades, however, some people are still determined to offer the hope of survival through shelters. In 1981 a group in La Verkin, Utah, called Survive Tomorrow, Inc., began a project of underground condominiums. According to the *Wall Street Journal*, the condominiums were directed toward groups known as "survivalists." The paper characterized these people, who expect catastrophe, as those who "buy gold, store food and supplies that will make them self-sufficient for long periods, purchase rifles and ammunition and acquire fortified homes in remote places." The president of the corporation said he hoped everyone would know how to use a gun.

The 226 windowless units were to be buried under 8 inches (20 cm) of concrete and 3.5 feet (107 cm) of dirt. The main entrance was to have a decontamination unit. A massive water-storage tank and generators for electricity were to be built. The units would be radiation proof, and air and water would be filtered for contamination. A one-bedroom unit would cost $39,000; a two-bedroom unit, $78,000. A four-year supply of food was to be included in the price. The corporation built two model units, and in 1981 had twelve commitments to buy. According to the corporation's president, the people who were interested expressed great concern about the nation's lack of civil defense planning. He concluded that if the government wouldn't do anything, private industry should.

CIVIL DEFENSE IN WESTERN EUROPE Most of Europe—as well as Great Britain—suffered tremendous damage to cities and civilian populations during World War II. Since that time most nations of Western Europe have tried to upgrade their civil defense programs—with varying degrees of success. As Dr. Eugene Wigner, an eminent physicist and proponent of a strong civil defense system, has pointed out, governments may plan for civil defense, but their citizens do not always agree with the planning.

Interestingly enough, the two nations with the most comprehensive civil defense programs are neutral—Sweden and Switzerland. Neutrality means that a nation does not take sides in a conflict—although it may lean toward one side or another. Its protection against more warlike neighbors is to secure its territory against attack.

Sweden has not been at war for more than 150 years. It does, however, have a military force designed to protect the country against invasion. Since Sweden does not expect to take a direct nuclear attack, the primary objective of its civil defense program is to protect its population from radioactive fallout. Because of its low population density, Sweden relies mainly on the evacuation of the urban populace to the countryside, where fallout would be less. Sweden's goal is to be able to evacuate as much as 90 percent of the urban population, for distances up to 250 miles.

Sweden has many underground, cave-like shelters; there is a total of fourteen of them located in the nine largest cities. But these are not intended to be used by the general population. Instead, they are to shelter the civil defense people who will carry on civil defense activities in case of war. Shelters do exist, however, to protect civilians from radioactive fallout.

Since the end of World War II, new commercial buildings are required to have reinforced concrete shelters with air-filtering systems. Sweden also stores critical supplies such as medicines and food underground. Essential defense industries, electric and water plants, and hospitals and schools also have underground shelters.

Civil defense in Sweden is coordinated by the national government and administered locally by provincial governors. All citizens between the ages of sixteen and sixty-five are subject to draft for civil defense service. From this pool, people are recruited and trained to staff emergency centers. Sweden has carried out exercises in evacuating and dispersing its urban population, and, under simulated conditions, the exercises have worked fairly well.

Probably Switzerland has the most highly organized civil defense system in the world. In fact, the Swiss have become civil defense instructors for many nations in Western Europe. In the early 1980s, in response to inquiries that poured into Switzerland for information on civil defense, the government set up a series of seminars dealing with modern warfare and protection. Britain, France, Italy, Spain, and Belgium have all requested information, along with many private firms.

Like their Swedish counterparts, Switzerland's civil defense planners do not think in terms of a direct nuclear attack. The Swiss are concerned with the possibility of war in a neighboring country, or the

These Swiss atomic air raid shelters were developed for use by the military as well as for civilians. The small shelters (*top*) are about 52 cubic feet (5¼ cubic meters) and hold three or four persons. The larger one (*below*) is about 270 cubic feet (27 cubic meters) and is built to accommodate twenty-two persons.

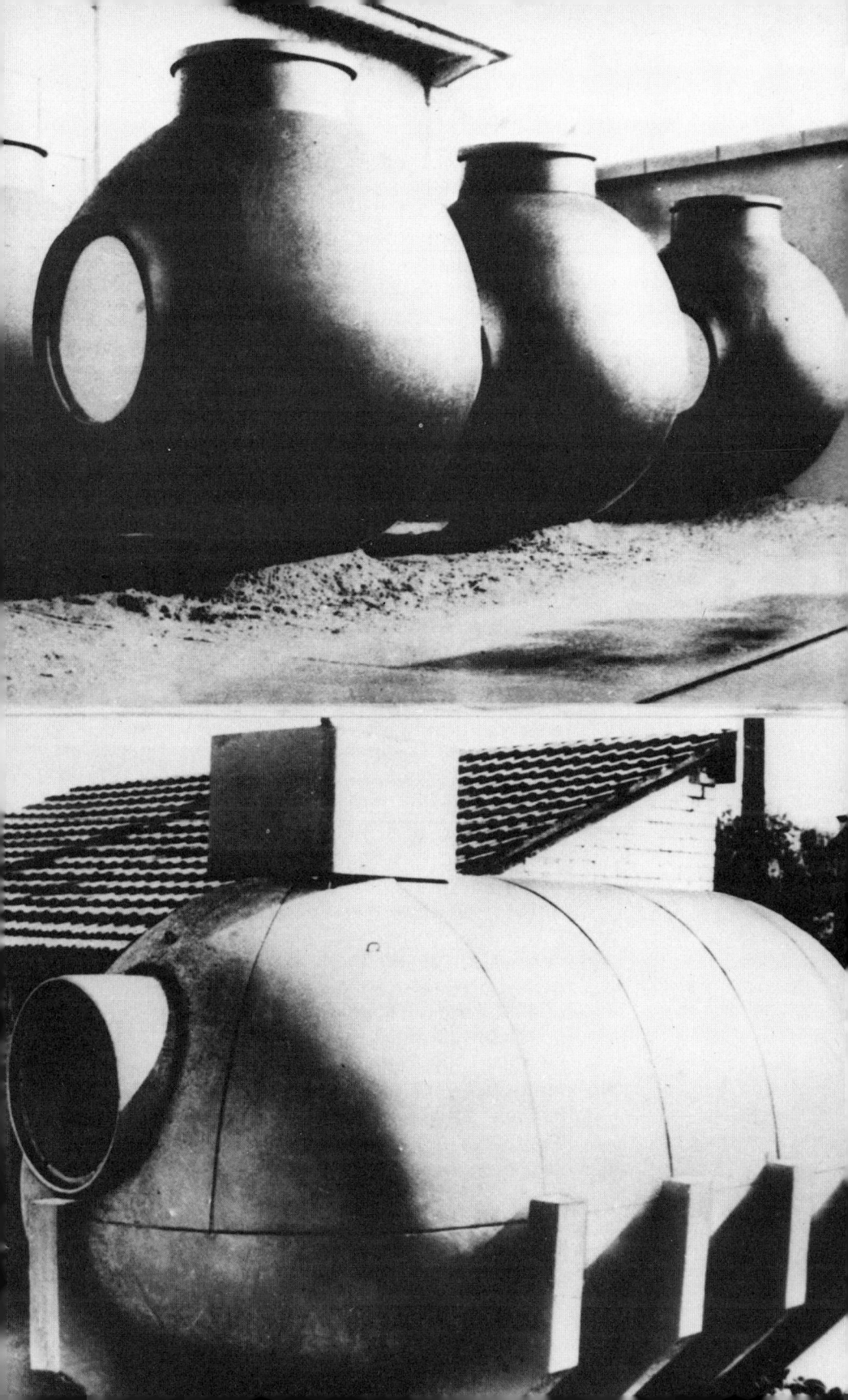

violation of their neutrality by an army crossing their territory to get to another country. Unlike Sweden, however, Switzerland emphasizes fallout shelters rather than evacuation. The shelters are designed to protect people against radiation and chemical weapons. Swiss shelters cannot take a direct hit by a nuclear weapon, but they can withstand substantial blast and heat waves.

Switzerland began to think of protecting its population in the early 1950s, shortly after the Korean War, but an overall strategy was not approved until the early 1960s. At that time the nation was in the midst of a building boom, and all new public and private buildings were required to have underground shelters. By 1963 a network of shelters, test alerts, and communications had been established.

Civil defense service is compulsory in Switzerland for men between the ages of twenty and sixty who are not on army duty. For women, service is voluntary. In 1981 the number of people involved in civil defense was about 250,000. The Swiss goal is to get a total of 625,000 into the system.

Switzerland's budget for civil defense is around $100 million a year. The various cantons (states) and local communities match government funds. The government also gives a 50 percent subsidy toward private shelters. It is estimated that by 1990, the civil defense budget will be nearly $3 billion.

Public shelters in Switzerland are equipped with generators and air filters that are easily operated. The doors are a foot (30.48 cm) thick and reinforced with two layers of steel. The shelters are regularly inspected and stocked with fresh supplies. They are designed for a fourteen-day stay, until the danger from radioactive fallout has decreased. The Swiss estimate that currently 90 percent of their population of 6.5 million would have the chance to survive a nuclear war, but by 1990, if all goes according to plan, there will be a shelter program for all civilians. It will include 1,000 underground hospitals and first-aid posts.

The Swiss have not yet had to use their shelters for emergencies. In the meantime, they have found some other, very practical uses for them. In some cities, public shelters have provided housing for youth groups, athletes, campers, and visiting orchestras. Private shelters have been turned into music rooms and gymnasiums. In Geneva one shelter is the meeting place for a wine-tasting society.

Switzerland and Sweden are neutral countries, and they do not possess nuclear weapons. Great Britain is different. As a nuclear power with offensive weapons, it is very likely to become a target in a nuclear war. Hence the British feel that a system of blast shelters would not provide adequate protection against an attack. Recently, though, a number of shelter-construction companies have sprung up in London. Some of them have shown interest in the Swiss shelter system.

However, Great Britain relies mainly on evacuating its people from urban areas and getting them dispersed around the countryside to presumably safer areas. British civil defense planners have set up a warning system in case of attack, at which point local police, fire fighters, and civil defense volunteers would put evacuation plans into operation.

Economic problems have prevented the British from spending much money on civil defense. The nation has a high rate of unemployment; industries such as coal mining, steel, and automobile manufacturing are declining. During the late 1970s and early 1980s, hundreds of factories and businesses closed down, and the country imported more than it exported. In addition, public attitudes toward civil defense range from apathy to outright hostility. The British antinuclear movement opposes a civil defense program on the grounds that there is no defense against nuclear war. In late 1983, despite vehement protest from such groups, the United States began placing nuclear missiles at American military bases in Great Britain. How this will affect the British civil defense program remains to be seen.

Like the United States, France expects a period of tension and crisis between nations before any nuclear attack would be launched. Then, France reasons, it will put its civil defense plans into effect. These plans call for the evacuation of populations from the cities and their dispersal over the countryside to safer places. To do this, France will use its police, fire, and health services. France had some experience in evacuating people during World War II. More than 3 million French people were successfully evacuated from areas occupied by the Germans into the unoccupied areas of the nation. Very little shelter construction has been done in France, but in Paris the subways could be used for shelter in case of a nuclear attack.

France has nuclear weapons, and it relies on these as a deterrent to attack. France also seems to feel that if it put a comprehensive civil defense plan into operation, such a move would lead the public and other nations to think the country's nuclear force was not very capable of defending the nation. Thus far in France, civil defense has not become a major issue, and plans have proceeded slowly.

West Germany is particularly vulnerable to nuclear attack, although it has no nuclear weapons of its own. And, although hundreds of Soviet missiles capable of carrying nuclear warheads are trained on the country, West Germany does not have an extensive civil defense system. For protection it tends to rely on what is called the "nuclear umbrella" of deterrence provided by the North Atlantic Treaty Organization (NATO). The NATO countries, including the United States, have set up a system of armed forces, bombers, submarines, and nuclear weapons in Western Europe. These are to protect Western Europe from the forces of the Soviet Union and its allies in Eastern Europe.

Controversy also surrounds West Germany's political and military role in the superpowers' arms race. More liberal governments in West Germany have downplayed a West German military role in the conflict between the United States and the Soviet Union. These governments have tried to reach a détente with the Soviet Union and with their Eastern European Communist neighbors. Recently, however, more conservative West German governments have anticipated playing a more active part in the struggle between East and West. A conservative government's decision to allow the United States to put nuclear missiles in West Germany is actively and militantly opposed by the nation's antinuclear groups. Representatives of these groups sit in the Bundestag (West Germany's parliament), and they oppose any further strengthening of Germany's military. West German defense policy is surrounded by controversy, and so is any planning for civil defense.

CAN CIVIL DEFENSE WORK?

"Everybody's going to make it if there are enough shovels to go around. Dig a hole and cover it with a couple of doors and then throw three feet of dirt on top of it. It's the dirt that does it." This statement by Thomas K. Jones, which appeared in the *Los Angeles Times* in January 1982, set off a storm of controversy.

"Who is this Thomas K. Jones who is saying those funny things about civil defense?" asked *The New York Times* in March 1982. "Is he only a character in 'Doonesbury'? . . . Or is T.K., as he is known to his friends, the peace movement's mole inside the Reagan administration?"

Thomas K. Jones is none of these. He is Deputy Under Secretary of Defense for Strategic Nuclear Forces, and he is the person who helped devise the blast test carried out by Boeing Aerospace in 1976 (see page 68). Jones also served as a member of the SALT II talks during the Ford administration. He is an ardent proponent of a massive civil defense buildup.

In 1976 Jones briefed Congress on civil defense and the Soviet buildup. He claimed that 98 percent of the Soviet population would survive an all-out attack by the United States. Furthermore, Jones said, the Soviet Union's industries could recover fully from such an attack in three to four years. This estimate, Jones said, was based on the premise that the Soviet Union has an extraordinary civil defense setup that is far superior to our own. Jones did explain at the time that his calculation of a 98 percent survival rate was predicated on the following theory: About three days before the Soviet Union was ready to attack the United States, Soviet civilians would leave the cities and head for the countryside, carrying the shovels they would need in order to dig shelters.

Around the same time that Jones was predicting the survival of the Soviet Union under an all-out attack, Paul H. Nitze was arguing that as the Soviets' civil defense program became more extensive, it was changing the policy of deterrence so carefully worked out by the United States and the Soviet Union. Nitze, also one of the negotiators of SALT II during the Nixon administration, argued that the Soviet Union was fortifying itself through its civil defense system. Hence, U.S. weapons were no longer enough of a threat to the Soviet population to deter an attack on the United States. In citing the imbalance, Nitze called for an upgrading and expansion of U.S. strategic weapons, and urged an all-out U.S. civil defense effort.

One of the ideas behind the SALT treaties was that if nuclear war threatened, the United States and the Soviet Union each would hold the other's population hostage. If, as some experts charged, the Soviets were now mounting a massive civil defense effort with the idea of fighting, winning, and surviving a nuclear war, the United States would be in a vulnerable position. Officials began to believe that the strategic balance between the United States and the Soviet Union was being upset.

Some experts asserted that there was not enough reliable data to show a huge civil defense buildup in the Soviet Union. One official, referring to T.K. Jones's estimate of Soviet civil defense, stated: "This whole thing has become a joke. The analysis just hasn't been done to justify any conclusions at all."

And Wolfgang Panofsky, an expert in nuclear technology, scoffed at Jones's picture of Soviet citizens digging shelters. "Those who . . . predict in detail that suddenly 100 million Soviets will all march out, build shelters which have a certain protection factor, have all these shelters beforehand stocked with food . . . simply rely on perfectly meaningless calculations which ignore the human element, which exists in the Soviet Union just as much as it does in the United States." The CIA, too, was skeptical of reports that Soviet civil defense efforts were large enough to threaten U.S. national security.

In 1976 and 1977 three government studies concluded that civil defense had little significance in the American-Soviet strategic balance. Another report studied

American and Soviet capabilities of inflicting damage. It concluded that although a Soviet buildup would reduce potential damage in a nuclear war, U.S. strategic weapons could still devastate the Soviet Union. The report also noted that a large-scale Soviet buildup would be detected and would serve to alert the United States to any impending attack. At the same time a Senate committee concluded that Soviet civil defense programs were not enough to upset the strategic balance between the two superpowers.

In the mid- and late 1970s, debate on civil defense also focused on how to deter an attack. Military strategists began to feel that a strong civil defense would do more than save lives if an attack occurred. It could, they argued, prevent an attack in the first place. Some national security people argued that without a strong civil defense, the United States would appear vulnerable to attack, and even invite it. Critics of this approach argued just the opposite. If the United States built a strong civil defense, they said, the Russians might think the Americans were preparing to launch a first strike and were getting ready to receive the retaliatory attack.

Still others considered the entire debate useless. They insisted that civil defense can never really protect populations and industries from attack. Bardyl Tirana, Carter's director of the Civil Defense Preparedness Agency, said: "It's folly to think of civil defense as being able to protect society as we know it from destruction in a very large-scale nuclear exchange." And Paul Warneke, director of the Arms Control and Disarmament Agency, said in 1978,

"Given the fact that we have in excess of 8,000 individually deliverable nuclear weapons, and the Soviet Union has maybe half that, you can't even find enough targets on which those nuclear warheads could usefully be employed. Now under those circumstances, I think, to talk about civil defense as enabling you to survive a nuclear war is indulging optimism to the point of total folly."

During this debate, the question of Soviet intent became a matter of disagreement. Those who wanted a stronger civil defense program as well as a buildup in arms argued that the Soviet Union might decide to evacuate its cities and then try to blackmail the United States into making economic or political concessions or else face an attack. Those who favored arms control argued that the Soviets did not have an indestructible civil defense system and knew that nuclear war would be suicide.

THE DEBATE CONTINUES

President Reagan's March 1982 call for a huge civil defense buildup heated up the debate over civil defense in a nuclear war. T.K. Jones's comments about shovels and dirt, which came at about the same time, helped to keep the debate going.

Arms control advocates, as well as those in the antinuclear and peace movements, condemn the whole plan. They contend that such a massive program indicates the government seriously thinks nuclear war is survivable. They say that the more flexibility the United States has in its strategic options, the more likely it will be to engage in nuclear war—and the less likely it will be to pursue meaningful arms negotiations.

Some critics of the plan think the program should be abandoned. They argue that any such massive commitment to civil defense makes nuclear war seem more palatable to the people. Some have pointed out that relocation in effect writes off large cities like New York and Los Angeles. There is no way, they argue, to get so many people out of these urban areas quickly. One critic declared that the United States is pursuing a dangerous policy because such a program tells people around the world that the United States is willing to fight a nuclear war.

The Reagan administration argues that there is a civil defense gap with the Soviet Union. Leon Gouré, along with T.K. Jones, supports the administration's plans. Gouré, a longtime civil defense advocate, argues that Soviet civil defense is better than the 1978 CIA study showed. Gouré, who directs Soviet studies for a firm in Virginia, believes that in the eyes of the Soviet leaders, a weak American civil defense signals a lack of U.S. will to fight.

ESCALATING THE ARMS RACE Most experts agree that the United States and the Soviet Union have enough nuclear warheads to destroy each other many times over. The United States can explode 12,000 nuclear weapons on the Soviet Union; the Soviet Union can explode 8,000 nuclear weapons on the United States. The United States is superior in the number of airborne and seaborne nuclear warheads it can deliver. About 50 percent of U.S. warheads are on submarine-based missiles; about 25 percent of the Soviet warheads are on submarine-based missiles. The Soviet Union is far superior in intercontinental, land-based missiles. However, the land-based missiles are becoming more and more vulnerable on both sides.

It is estimated that the total number of weapons possessed by both sides is 50,000. U.S. warheads could be delivered to the Soviet Union by the U.S. "triad" of strategic weapons. These are the land-based missiles, the submarine-based missiles, and those launched by strategic bombers. About two-thirds of the U.S. submarines are on patrol in the open ocean, making them nearly invulnerable to attack. Twenty-seven percent of U.S. warheads are carried on bombers. One-third of these bombers are on alert at all times, ready for rapid take-off. The remainder of U.S. warheads are on land-based intercontinental ballistic missiles. They are in fixed locations and are more vulnerable to a Soviet strike.

In comparison, Soviet strategic forces are less evenly distributed, with a heavy preponderance of land-based intercontinental ballistic missiles. These are also fixed in silos. About 25 percent of Soviet warheads are carried on submarines.

At the end of 1983, the Reagan administration began setting up, in Great Britain and West Germany, the first of the 108 Pershing II ballistic missiles and 464 ground- and sea-launched missiles it plans to install in Western Europe. At the same time the government was planning to add a deep underground base for the MX land-based missiles, to make them less vulnerable to attack. The secretary of defense also ordered the military services to integrate their plans for using medium- and long-range nuclear weapons in order to fight a war more efficiently.

In response to U.S. plans to deploy missiles in Europe, a Soviet official announced in October 1983 that the Soviet Union would station its own new missiles in places from which they would be able to reach the United States within ten minutes of launching. (He did not say exactly where these would be stationed, although he did rule out Cuba.) The same official said that when the United States set up missiles in Europe, the Soviet Union would break off the disarmament talks on intermediate-range weapons that had been going on in Geneva, Switzerland, between the two superpowers. Positioning medium-range missiles in Europe is a new development in the arms race. The Soviet Union has claimed many times that it has no medium-range nuclear missiles outside its own territory. The Soviets claim that the U.S. missiles in Europe can reach their territory in eight to ten minutes. They say that the planned deployment of their own missiles outside the Soviet Union is meant to overcome this U.S. advantage.

ARE FEMA'S ASSUMPTIONS VALID?

Few people would argue over the value of civil defense in peacetime disasters. Government planning to meet emergencies such as floods, earthquakes, fires, and so forth is a well-organized program. With government planning and help, local communities over the years have been able to cope with a variety of disasters and survive.

When it comes to civil defense in planning for war and as a deterrent to war, especially nuclear war, the critics are vehement in their opposition. Most critics are unanimous in not accepting FEMA's assumption that 80 percent of the population would survive. They contend that FEMA's calculations are totally unrealistic. They point to FEMA's premise that there will be an escalation in tension and crisis before an attack, so that people will have some warning time. This conjecture assumes the Soviets will launch a first strike, which is not certain. It also assumes that the United States would somehow know about it hours, days, or perhaps a week ahead of time. FEMA admits that this is conjecture but points to the Soviet evacuation plans, which are based on the same premise.

Another objection is that FEMA's figures are not the same as those given by other government agencies. Carla Johnston, director of New Century Policies, in Cambridge, Massachusetts, notes that FEMA says 40 million will be killed. But the Office of Technology Assessment has a different figure—150 million. Johnston also recalls an estimate made even earlier by Robert McNamara, secretary of defense in the Johnson administration. When he was asked how many casualties the United States could sustain before it would cease to exist as a modern nation, he replied 50 to 55 million.

Many critics find it disturbing that FEMA seems to try to present its survival figures in a positive light. FEMA seldom refers to the number of people killed, talking instead of survival rates. FEMA's estimate of the number who will die is 20 percent. That is about 45 million people. Many opponents of civil defense are particularly critical of FEMA's apparent assumption that no deaths will occur among the people who have left the cities under its crisis-relocation plans. FEMA, they claim, has ignored the fact of radiation sickness and other nuclear-related illnesses among these people.

Radiation levels will be high in many areas, and the types of protection given may be of no use at all. Most studies show that, depending on the weather and wind patterns, radiation can drift for hundreds of miles before falling back to earth.

FEMA does recognize the fallout problem. Its plans call for all evacuees and residents of host areas to have fallout protection. It admits that as of now, however, the facilities existing in the host areas are inadequate, even for the local residents. Hence, according to FEMA, people would be obliged to dig or construct their own shelters. Under the best of conditions, the critics say, that would be a nearly impossible task. It takes 18 inches (46 cm) of dirt piled against walls and windows to reduce radiation tenfold. People escaping from a nuclear blast are not apt to be in good enough condition to make such shelters.

People must also remain inside shelters until the fallout declines to an acceptable level, so a shelter must have air, sanitation facilities, and food. It should also have medical supplies and, if possible, protective clothing. One FEMA booklet instructs people to bring nonperishable food with them. FEMA also claims there will be food in stores in the host area. And for the long term, retailers would have to change their wholesale-to-retail distribution plans. FEMA's long-term food plans would depend almost entirely on commercial distributors.

Civil defense critics argue that following a nuclear attack, there will be no such things as food-distribution plans. Cities will be destroyed, the transportation system in a shambles, and the ground contaminated by fallout. Livestock will be dead or useless for food; crops will be inedible. How, ask the critics, can there be anything like a normal system of distribution?

They also point out what they feel is one of the most erroneous assumptions about the 80 percent survival-rate figure—the failure of the plans to deal with the fate of the evacuees beyond the so-called shelter period. Scientists and physicians have pointed out that a large number of people will die within months of leaving the shelters. The deaths will be the result of conditions in the postattack world. The nation's medical facilities would be gone or incapacitated. An enemy would no doubt have targeted critical stockpiles of medicines, fuel, and stored foods. And there is no assurance that there would be any administrators to allocate goods. Housing would be destroyed; electric power would probably be lost. In effect, the critics say, civil defense may protect some lives, but it cannot prevent the widespread destruction of property and materials necessary to keep life going.

Some scientists have painted a grim picture of spreading disease, as unsanitary conditions and malnutrition weaken people's resistance. Without adequate medical supplies or sanitation, massive public-health problems would occur.

Almost all critics scoff at the idea of 150 million people attempting to leave the major cities across the country all at once.

It would, they claim, bring all movement to a complete standstill. In answer to the statement that 50 million Americans leave cities every weekend, critics point to the massive traffic jams that result. In Washington, D.C., FEMA plans call for city bus drivers to take out those people who do not have cars. The drivers are to make three round-trips to and from distant locations. Writing in the *Michigan Quarterly Review*, Arthur Vander questions FEMA's assumption that a driver would take his wife and family on the first trip and then turn around and leave them two more times to go back to a city that will be demolished. Another supposition questioned by critics is that the behavior of those who are to carry out crisis relocation will be the same in a nuclear attack as it is in peacetime disasters. No local flood or fire, they say, is at all comparable to a nuclear attack.

Another issue that FEMA does not address is the behavior of the enemy while all this is going on. In a list of "Ten Illusions of Civil Defense," physicians Jack Geiger and Eric Chivian note that even if evacuation were successful, the Soviet Union could merely retarget its missiles to the host areas. Mass evacuation, according to FEMA, would take at least three days. The Soviets can retarget missiles in fractions of that time.

Some of FEMA's instructions do seem a bit odd. One set of instructions given to the residents of Plattsburgh, New York, advises the people to "Prepare Now. . . . Check to see if you live in the risk area. . . . Check your route assignment and route map. . . . Check your home for security. See that all locks are secure.

Close all window shades, blinds and drapes." For people who cannot leave, such as those in hospitals, the instructions advise: "If you are in a hospital (or any institution) you will be evacuated. Patients who cannot be removed because of special requirements will be sheltered and cared for in case of imminent attack." But the instructions do not say how.

The opponents of civil defense paint a dark picture of nuclear attack and the inability of civil defense to deal with it. But those who are responsible for the nation's security see civil defense as something of an insurance plan—the more preparations we make today, the better our chances of surviving a nuclear war if it should come tomorrow.

THE FUTURE OF CIVIL DEFENSE

No one can predict what the future of civil defense in the United States will be. As the antinuclear debate goes on, more and more people may decide that massive civil defense is not a workable plan in the nuclear age, and that it is not a substitute for arms negotiations.

Some communities across the nation have refused to take part in FEMA's civil defense planning. In Boulder, Colorado, shortly after the program was announced, angry residents met and rejected the agency's plan for evacuating the Boulder area. The vote was broadcast on television and brought in floods of mail from coast to coast.

Shortly after the Boulder vote, the Sacramento, California, county board of supervisors passed a resolution denouncing civil defense. The board called for more nuclear arms limitation talks. They also refused to allocate funds for civil defense, saying that county funds were not "to be diverted toward crisis relocation" because "no meaningful social survival will be possible under any circumstances following a nuclear attack."

In Greensboro, North Carolina, the director of the local civil defense program publicly expressed her doubts about the usefulness of civil defense and then asked that all fallout shelter signs in the city be removed. Houston, Texas, has just about stopped all civil defense preparations. The assistant director of civil defense said that the Houston highway system was antiquated, and that with two million residents to evacuate, crisis relocation was not feasible.

The Office of Technology Assessment study on the effects of a nuclear attack on Detroit points up the likelihood of terrible damage to urban areas, and the unlikelihood that people could get out of the city. In San Diego, California, the head of the county civil defense office explained that there was no place for the residents to go. "We can't go south into Mexico, west into the Pacific Ocean or north toward Los Angeles, so the only way out is east. And once you cross the mountains, you're in the desert."

In the foreseeable future, the chances for arms limitation do not seem too bright. Each escalation on one side brings a further escalation on the other. The United States is determined to spread its missiles over Western Europe, and the Soviets are determined to respond. And President Reagan's recent proposal to put defensive arms into space has raised new questions about any nation's ability to defend its territory.

The issue of civil defense is a complex one. Each side in the debate is concerned over the fate of the United States. Those who want an expanded weapons system want the nation to be protected, and they believe strongly that civil defense is a major factor in getting that protection. The opponents of civil defense also want to protect the country, but they believe civil defense and more arms will have the opposite effect. For them, outlawing nuclear weapons and reducing the arms race is the only answer.

FOR FURTHER INFORMATION

Information on civil defense can be found in magazines, newspapers, and journals. Engineering and scientific journals tend to deal with the technical aspects of civil defense, such as the advantages or disadvantages of certain kinds of shelters. The U.S. government publishes handbooks on civil defense, but not all of them are up-to date. The 1978 CIA report, *Soviet Civil Defense* (referred to on page 61), is available from the Library of Congress. FEMA has an extensive catalog of its publications, many of which are directed toward workers in the civil defense field. But local FEMA offices also have handbooks describing FEMA and its programs, and also civil defense pamphlets detailing the procedures to take in emergencies. One of the pamphlets is *What You Should Know about Nuclear Preparedness.*

Survival and the Bomb, by Eugene Wigner (University of Indiana Press, Bloomington, 1969), is a collection of essays on methods of civil defense, and it includes some technical material. Wigner is a proponent of civil defense.

The main independent advocacy group for civil defense is the American Civil Defense Association in Stark, Florida. It publishes the *Journal of Civil Defense*, a bimonthly magazine.

Antinuclear groups that also concern themselves with civil defense issues are Physicians for Social Responsibility, the Union of Concerned Scientists, and the Center for Defense Information. They publish newsletters and other literature on the antinuclear movement and the arms race.

The Fate of the Earth, by Jonathan Schell (Alfred A. Knopf, New York, 1982), describes in detail a full-scale nuclear war and the possible extinction of humanity. *The Day after World War III*, by Edward Zuckerman (Viking Press, New York, 1984), recounts the American government's plans for fighting and recovering from a nuclear war.

The Stanley Foundation in Muscatine, Iowa, has produced a cassette tape on civil defense as part of its *Common Ground* series. The tape is a lively debate between an official of FEMA and some opponents of civil defense.

INDEX

Page numbers in italics indicate illustrations.

Airborne command posts, 69
Airplanes, *18*, 19
　spotting of, 22, 24, 25
Air raids, 9, 21-22, *23*, 24-26
American Civil War, 16-17
American Telephone and Telegraph, 67-68
Andrews Air Force Base, 69
Antiballistic missile systems (ABMs), 48-49
Antinuclear movement, 80, 82, 87
Arms control, 38, 47, 87, 97
Arms Control and Disarmament Agency, 52, 70, 86
Arms limitation. *See* Arms control
Arms race, 2, 47-48, 52, 81, 87, 90, 97, 98
Atomic bombs, 2, 8, 11-12, 27, 29, 61
Atomic Energy Act, 35
Atomic Energy Commissions, 34, 36

Berlin Wall, 41
Blackouts, 22, 25-26
Blast protection, 41-42, 44, 50, 54. *See also* Shelters, blast
Boeing Aerospace, 68-69
Boston, Mass., 71
Boulder, Colo., 96
Brecht, Bertolt, 16
Brezhnev, Leonid, *51*
Budget requests, 30, 38, 39, 41, 42, 49, 52, 53, 65, 96
Budestag, 82
Burns, 6, 9, 11

Cancer, 11
Cars as shelters, 70
Carter, Jimmy, 50, *51*, 53, 86
Carthage, 14
Central Intelligence Agency (CIA), 61-63, 65, 71, 85, 88
Central locator system, 70
Children, 11, 37
Civil Air Patrol, 26
Civil defense, defined, 1
Civil defense, history of, 1-3
　in 1950s, 27-39

101

Civil defense, history (cont.)
   in 1960s, 39–48
   in 1970s, 48–53
   in 1980s, 53–59, 87–95
Civil defense objectives, 54, 61–62, 75, 78–80
Civil Defense Preparedness Agency, 86
Civil defense service, 76, 78
Civilian Air Warning System, 24
Civilians, 1–2, 5, 13–17, 19–20, 25, 43, 62
Civil War. See American Civil War
Clothing, 34, 64, 92
Coastal patrols, 26
Cockroaches, 43
Cold war politics, 63–64
Cost of civil defense, 52–53, 56, 63, 65, 78. See also Budget requests; Funding, government
Council of National Defense, 20
Coventry, England, 22
Crisis relocation, 37, 57–58, 71, 92, 94, 97. See also Evacuation
Cuba, 90
Cuban missile crisis, 39–42
Death rates, 4, 6, 8, 11, 19, 27, 37, 43. See also Survival rate
Détente, 48, 49, 81
Deterrence, 84, 86, 90
Detroit, Mich., 5–6, 7, 8, 97
Disarmament talks, 48, 87, 90, 96
Disaster Assistance Center, 59
Distribution of supplies, 70, 72, 92–93
Drills, 32, *33*

Economic systems, 4, 62, 70. See also Industrial protection
"The Effects of Nuclear War," 4–8
Einstein, Albert, 36–37
Eisenhower, Dwight, 29, 36, 38, 39
Escalation. See Arms race

Estonia, 64
Evacuation, 20, 21, 37, 42, 50, 52, 54–55, 57–58, 70–72, 88, 93–94
   in France, 80
   in Soviet Union, 63, 70–71, 84, 87, 91
   in Sweden, 75–76
   See also Crisis relocation

Fallout, 6, 36–37, 43, 92
Federal Civil Defense Administration (FCDA), 29, 38
Federal Emergency Management Agency (FEMA), 52–59, 65, 71, 90–92, 94, 96
Food distribution, 45, 70, 72, 92–93
Ford, Gerald, 49, 84
France, 80–81
Funding, government, 29–30, 41, 49, 52, 54, 56, 59

Georgia, 16–17
Germany, 15, 19
Germany, West, 81–82, 89
Government, continuity of, 53, 62–63, 69
Government leaders, 62–63, 69
Government secrecy, 35–36
Government studies, 85–86. See also Central Intelligence Agency
Grass roots involvement, 66
Great Britain, 19, 21, 79–80, 89
Greensboro, N.C., 97
Ground zero, 5, 8

Heart disease, 11
Hibakusha, 11
Hiroshima, 8–9, *10*, 11–12, 27, *28*
Host communities, 57
Houston, Tex., 97
"How to Survive an Atomic Bomb," 32
Hydrogen bomb, 35–38

Industries, protection of, 54, 64, 65, 67–69, 75

102

Injuries, 5, 8. *See also* Burns
Intercontinental missiles, 88–89

Japan. *See* Hiroshima; Nagasaki; Tokyo
Jericho, 13–14
Johnson, Lyndon, 91
Jones, Thomas K., 83–85, 88

Kahn, Herman, 37
Kennedy, John, 39, *40*
Korean War, 27, 29

La Guardia, Fiorello, 24
Lawrence Radiation Laboratory, 44
Leadership. *See* Government leaders; Workers, civil defense
Leukemia, 11
Life span, 11
Limited nuclear war, 49–50, 52–53
Lithuania, 64
Little Boy, 9, *10*
Local governments, 20, 25–26, 29, 39, 54, 59, 73, 76, 78
Los Angeles, Cal., 88

McNamara, Robert, 91
Mental retardation, 11
Middle Ages, 14–15
Morale, 20, 22–24
"Mother Courage and her Children," 16
Mount Weather, 38, 69
Mutual assured destruction (MAD), 47–48, 65
MX land-based missiles, 89

Nagasaki, 11–12
National Emergency Control Center, 67–68
National Security Council, 29
Negotiations. *See* Disarmament talks
Neutrality, 74, 79
New Century Policies, 91
New York, N.Y., 71, 88

Nixon, Richard, 49, 84
North Atlantic Treaty Organization (NATO), 81
Nuclear test ban treaty, 47. *See also* Strategic Arms Limitation Treaty
Nuclear umbrella, 81
Nuclear warheads, 38, 88, 89

Occupancy tests, 45–46
Office of Civil Defense, 24–26
Office of Civil Defense Mobilization, 39
Office of Technology Assessment (OTA), 4, 91, 97
Ohio, *33*, 71
"On the Beach," 32, 34
Opinion polls, 43–44

Pauling, Linus, 37
Pearl Harbor, 25
Pentagon, 41, 52
Pershing II missiles, 89
Philadelphia, Penn., 71
Physical defects, 11, 37
Plattsburgh, N.Y., 94–95
President, U.S., 69–79
Public attitude, 39, 44, 66, 80. *See also* Antinuclear movement
Public health, 93

Radiation, *See* Fallout
Radio, Soviet, 63–64, 67
Reagan, Ronald, 53–54, 87–89, 97
Relocation. *See* Evacuation
Risk areas, 57–58

Sacramento, Cal., 96
SALT Treaties. *See* Strategic Arms Limitation Treaty
San Diego, Cal., 97
Shelters,
    air raid, 21–22, *23*, 24–25, 37, *77*
    blast, 44, 54, 62–63, 73
    fallout, 41, 44–47, 58–59, 63, 70, 73, 75, 78
    home, 30–32, 37, 58–59, 73, 74

Soviet, *60*, 62–63, 67, 69, 70–71, 73
Swiss, *77*, 78–79
trench, 31, 37
See also Underground facilities
Sherman, General William T., 16–17
Shock wave, 9
Shute, Nevil, 32
Silos, 89
Soviet-American relations, 27, 37, 41–42, 47–48. *See also* Cold war; Détente; Disarmament talks
Soviet civil defense evacuation plans, 63, 70–71
leadership, 62–63, 69
objectives, 61–62
personnel, 65–66
threat to U.S., 84–87
See also Shelters
Soviet missile threat. *See* Cuban missile crisis
Space and weapons, 47, 97
Sputnik, 38
Stanford Research Institute, 71
State governments, 20, 25, 29, 39, 54, 59, 78
Stevenson, Adlai, 38
Stockpiling, 30, 58, 75, 78
Strategic Arms Limitation Treaty (SALT I), 48–49, 85
Strategic Arms Limitation Treaty (SALT II), 49, 51, 84, 85
Strategic balance, 84–86
Strategic weapons, 48, 84, 86, 89
Submarines, 69, 88–89
Submarine watches, 26
Subways as shelters, 19, 23, *32*, 80
Survivable nuclear war, 65, 70, 72, 79, 83, 85, 87, 95
Survival, 11–12, 37, 43–46, 65, 72, 92–93, 97
Survival Associates, 44, 46
Survival rate, 54, 79, 84, 91, 93
Survive Tomorrow, 73
Sweden, 75–76
Switzerland, 78–79

Tanks, World War I, *18*
Targeting policy, 52–53
"Ten Illusions of Civil Defense," 94
Tests, nuclear, 43, 47
Thirty Year War, 15
TNT equivalent, 9, 10, 12
Tokyo, 8
Topographic effects, 5
Transportation, 70–72
Treaty. *See* Nuclear test-ban treaty; Strategic Arms Limitation Treaty
Trench warfare, 19
Triad of Weapons, 89
Truman, Harry, 29

Ukraine, 64
Underground facilities, 67, 69, 72–75, 79, 89. *See also* Shelters
U.S. nuclear missiles in Europe, 80, 82, 89–90
Warheads. *See* Nuclear warheads
Warning signs, 58, 86–87, 91
Warning time, 55, 63, 69–71, 80, 84, 91
Washington, D.C., 69, 71, 94
alternate site for, 38
Weapons, 15, 17, *18*, 19
Weapons, nuclear, 87–90
U.S. in Europe, 80, 82, 89–90. *See also* antiballistic missile systems; Intercontinental missiles; MX land-based missiles; Nuclear warheads; Pershing II ballistic missiles
West Germany. *See* Germany, West
Wilson, Woodrow, 21
Winnable nuclear war, 53
Workers, civil defense, 21–22, 24–25, 54–55, 62, 66, 68, 75–76, 78–80
World War I, 2, 18–19
World War II, 2, 21–26

X rays, 43